CHINESE ZODIAC SIGNS

CHINESE ZODIAC SIGNS

YEAR OF THE SNAKE

1905 · 1917 · 1929
1941 · 1953 · 1965
1977 · 1989 · 2001

ARROW

Arrow Books Limited
17-21 Conway Street, London W1P 6JD
An imprint of the Hutchinson Publishing Group
London Melbourne Sydney Auckland
Johannesburg and agencies throughout the world
First published by M.A. Editions 1982
Arrow edition 1984
© M.A. Editions 1982

Produced by Aurum Press, 33 Museum Street, London WC1
Original text in French by Catherine Aubier
Translated by Eileen Finletter and Ian Murray
Designed by Julie Francis
Phototypeset in Optima
by York House Typographic, Hanwell, London
Made and printed in Great Britain
by Anchor Brendon Limited, Tiptree, Essex

ISBN 0 09 933470 4

CONTENTS

In the same series

HOW TO USE THIS BOOK

Each section of this book gives a detailed description of the character, personality and partnership possibilities of the Snake. The characteristics of this sign are described in conjunction with the important ascendant sign.

There is also a synthesis of the Chinese zodiac and the more familiar Western zodiac. Together these give new meaning and depth to the description and prediction of an individual's personality, the main tendencies of his character, his behaviour and the broad outline of his destiny.

The book concludes with the fascinating astrological game, the I Ching.

The arrangement of the book is as follows:

A short introduction to the background and philosophy of the Chinese zodiac (page 8).

A description of the characteristics of your specific Chinese sign, determined by the *year of your birth* — in this case the Snake (page 19).

The best (and worst) partners for that Sign, determined by *the hour of your birth* (page 42).

The combination and interaction of your sign with the Ascendant Element: Earth, Water, Fire, Wood, Metal (page 51).

The comparison and combination of the two zodiacs — Chinese and Western (for example, the Sagittarian Snake, the Virgo Snake) — highlight many subtleties which enable you to clarify your psychological portrait (page 68).

The astrological game of the I Ching, which adapts the ancient Taoist 'Book of Mutations' to each Chinese sign. This simple game offers the reader the opportunity to obtain wise and appropriate answers to abstract as well as everyday questions (page 77).

THE MYSTERIES OF CHINESE ASTROLOGY

中國星相
學之神秘

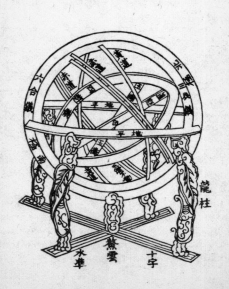

The legend of Buddha

One Chinese New Year more than five centuries before Christ, Buddha invited all the animals in creation to come to him, promising them recompense appropriate to his all-powerful and miraculous kindness and generosity. However, dimmed by their preoccupations of the moment (is it not said in the West that the characteristic of the animal is merely to eat, sleep, couple and fear?), almost all of them ignored the call of the Divine Sage. Yet twelve of the animals did go to him. They were, in order of their arrival, the Rat, Ox, Tiger, Rabbit, Dragon, Snake, Horse, Goat, Monkey, Rooster, Dog and Pig (other traditions replace the Rabbit with the Cat and the Pig with the Wild Boar).

To thank them Buddha offered each a year which would be dedicated to him alone through the ages. This year would carry the animal's name, and express his symbolic character and his specific psychological traits, marking the personality and behaviour of people born during that year.

Thus a cycle of twelve years was established, fitting exactly the sequence and rhythm of this improbable bestiary (one can imagine the dizzying amount of work which would have faced the astrologer if all of the animals had answered Buddha's invitation!).

Such is the legend.

The lunar cycle

Actually, Chinese astrology precedes the development of Far Eastern Buddhism, which began only in the 5th century of the Christian era, or about one thousand years after Buddha's appearance on earth. However, astrologers were already practising their art in China ten centuries before Christ; but the very origins of this astrology are as controversial as they are immemorial.

One point cannot be disputed: contrary to the West, which developed a solar astrology based on the apparent displacements of the daily star as its position in the Western zodiac changed from month to month, the Far East constructed a lunar astrology based on the annual cycle of lunar movements. This is why the Asian New Year — the Tet celebration among the Vietnamese — never falls exactly on the same date (page 93).

While the phases of the moon are equally important for a Western astrologer, their context is inscribed differently, with the result that their play of correspondence — and so their meanings and implications — are not comparable to those of Eastern astrology.

Without entering too deeply into scientific considerations which would lead us away from the purposes of this book, let us simply remind ourselves of the obvious and multiple influences of the moon, for example the movement of the tides, as well as more subtle levels, such as the female cycles and the obscure depths of the psyche. The term 'lunatic' has a precise and, indeed, clinical meaning. Recent statistical studies, for example, have made it possible to establish a strange and significant increase in acts of violence and criminality on nights when there is a full moon. Also, rigorous tests have established the direct impact of the moon on the chemical composition of certain bodies whose molecular structure can be modified depending on whether or not they have been exposed to lunar light.

Nuances of Chinese astrology

So, here we are with our twelve animals, the *Emblems* of Chinese astrology. Does this mean that all persons born in the same year as, say, the Rat or the Horse, will be subject to the same formulae of character and destiny? No more so than that those born under the sign of Aries or Libra are all confined to the same zodiacal script.

In Western astrology, the position of the planets, the calculation of the Ascendant and the Golden Mean of the Sky and its Mansions, allows the astrologer to refine and individualize a given theme considerably. In the same way, in Chinese astrology one obtains some surprisingly detailed and complex results. This is achieved by integrating with the intitial data factors such as the *Companion in Life* (determined by the hour of birth, but not to be confused with the Western Ascendant), and the predominant *Element*, which refers to the five Elements: Earth, Water, Fire, Wood and Metal.

This triple point of view — the *Emblematic Animal*, the *Companion in Life* and the *Element* — provide the reader with a greater diversity of references and a totality of perspectives both more rich and more precise than those found in Western astrology. To this we have added a detailed interpretation of the relationship between the Chinese and Western signs. The two astrologies are by nature distinct but never contradictory, and therefore complementary aspects and fusion can only result in a more profound understanding of the psychological types emanating from them. However, it is important to stress that although the concept of analogy holds an important place in Chinese astrology, it bears neither the same sense nor the same overall significance as in Western astrology.

Each Chinese sign is a universe in itself, a small cosmos

with its own laws and domains, completely independent of all other signs. Each of these living creatures is given specific powers and functions, becoming an emblematic animal endowed with a particular dimension peculiar unto itself. It creates its own jungle or cavern, and defines by its rhythm its own cadences and breathing. In this way it secretes its own chemistry — or, rather, its own alchemy. It is a supple, mobile, fluctuating image, governed by its own internal metamorphoses and contradictions.

Once we understand this, we will see that it is fatal to impose a fixed framework or clearly circumscribed area of mental categories and psychological equations in order to protect or reassure an anguished ego seeking a comforting or flattering projection of its own desires and fears.

Our alignment to a Chinese sign cannot be defined by exclusive formulae or linear classifications. The Chinese symbol unfolds slowly, a gift of the Gods, of Time and of Mystery; a delectable or poisoned gift which an Oriental person accepts with humility because he knows that its flavour may be born of the poison, as its poison may be born of the flavour.

Sometimes, in the course of a lifetime, it is circumstances more than a character trait which seem to determine and crystallize the principal tendencies of a sign. In such cases a thread of major or minor events will tend to form a symphonic background to the style of, say, a Dragon or a Rat.

To Have and To Be

Through the centuries Chinese astrology has permeated and inspired the mental attitudes and behaviour of hundreds of millions of people in the Far East, to an extent that is difficult for us to accept or even appreciate.

To understand better the spirit in which these people rely on the art of contemplation in handling the problems of daily life, a cardinal point must be emphasized — one which probably constituted the essential and fundamental difference between Eastern and Western civilizations, and poses a virtually impassable dividing line between them.

In our Western 'consumer society' — irrespective of the admiring or negative feelings we may associate with this expression — the fundamental question, from birth to death and at all levels of activity, is: 'What can I have?'. We are continuously asking what we might possess or enjoy; what material goods, fortune, luck, honours or power might be had; whether we will achieve success in love, prestige, a good job, family, health, home, friends or, on another level, culture and knowledge. It is always a question of, 'What can I obtain, preserve, enlarge?' which underlies the totality of our motivations.

Think of the *models* that are held up to us: the successful politicians, business tycoons, film and stage stars, celebrated artists or scientist, sports champions, heroes of crime novels or comic strips. Idols of all kinds incarnate the triumph and glory of 'to have'. All will say, 'I have the most power, the most money, the most diplomas and abilities', or even, 'Mine is the greatest love affair'. Or, why not 'Mine is the most terrible drama, the most frightful illness'? Esteem is won exclusively from what one *has*.

Still more obvious is advertising, which is omnipresent today, and proclaims that one must absolutely *have* such and such a product in order *to be:* dynamic, seductive, happy, at ease with oneself or wholly fulfilled.

For Orientals, the decisive question is not 'What can I have?' but 'Whom can I be?' The model aspired to is not the great leader, the hero or the champion, but the poor, naked Sage who has attained total freedom and perfect peace within himself. Princes and great businessmen bow low before him, for he is the image of the highest self-realization possible to man. In this perspective, the Sage renounces nothing; on the contrary, since he has attained the supreme reality, he is immeasurably richer than the most powerful ruler.

It is we who, due to our fragmented and illusory

attachments, our infantile whims and our incessant conflicts, continually forgo the most marvellous felicity of all — God.

'*Who am I?*' Whatever approaches and methods, schools, sects or forms of asceticism are followed, this question, in appearance so simple and banal, lies at the base of and is the key to all Oriental culture. Through it lies the way to true liberation, by way of those roads to genuine understanding and knowledge known as Yoga, Vedanta, Tantra, Tao and Zen — to cite only the best known.

All this may cause the Chinese approach to astrology to seem disconcerting to us. The Oriental does not think '*I have* such and such predispositions, aptitudes or weaknesses inherent in my horoscope', but rather, 'How can I *be* a Rat (or a Goat or a Dog) in all the circumstances of my life?'

The Oriental's goal is not 'to have' in the same way in which we in the West say 'I possess such and such a quality or defect'. For him, it is instead a question of directions, implying a subtle and rhythmic progression; a sort of poetic dance of destiny, with each animal possessing its own steps and pirouettes — an entire choreography of its own.

These subtleties must be perceived clearly by those who wish to evolve without losing their way or turning round in circles in this immense domain of shimmering and shifting aspects of understanding.

The astrological I Ching

In the last section of this book, we present a game inspired by the oracles of the I Ching and adapted to each sign.

In his book *Zen Buddhism*, Alan Watts wrote: 'The I Ching is a work of divination containing oracles based on 64 abstract figures, each composed of six traits. These traits are of two sorts: divided or negative and undivided or positive. A modern psychologist would recognize an analogy with the Rorschach test, whose aim is to establish the mental portrait of an individual according to the spontaneous images suggested to him by an inkspot or an over-elaborate design. A subject whose images are inspired by the inkspot should be able to use his subsequent perceptions to deduce the necessary practical information to guide his future behaviour. Considered in this way, the divinatory art of the I Ching cannot be attacked as a vulgar superstition.'

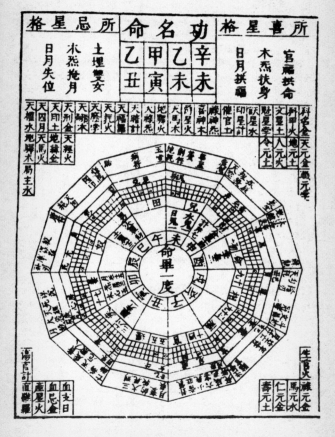

The relationship between the Signs and the Lunar Mansions

THE SNAKE

The practitioner of the I Ching commands an entire critical survey of the methods available when important decisions have to be made. We, on the other hand, are convinced that our decisions are rational because we depend upon a cluster of valid data affecting a problem; not for us to leave it to a mere game of heads or tails. The practitioner, however, might question whether we know what information is truly valid, given the fact that our plans are being constantly upset by events which are wholly unpredictable. Indeed, if we were rigorously rational in our choices of the data upon which our behaviour depended, so much time would be required that the moment for action would pass before we could assemble the data. Although we may set out initially to seek this information in a scientific manner, we are rapidly forced to act on another basis — capricious intuition, the impossibility of thinking further because we are too exhausted, or simply that time is too short and a choice must be made. In other words, our most important decisions are based largely on impressions, on our capacity to 'feel' a situation.

Every practitioner of the I Ching knows this. He is aware that his method is not an exact science but a useful and effective approach, if he is endowed with sufficient powers of intuition or, as he would say, 'in the Tao'.

THE YIN AND THE YANG

The *Yin* and the *Yang* are the symbols of two opposing and complementary principles whose indissoluble play and constant metamorphosis represent the roots, indeed the very tissues of the universe in action. They represent the eternal opposites — Positive-Negative, Yes-No, White-Black, Day-Night, Full-Empty, Active-Passive, Masculine-Feminine, and so on. Each contains within itself the germ of the other. That is why the man (Yang) bears within himself a feminine component (Yin), and the woman (Yin) a masculine one (Yang).

The Yin-Yang coupling is both indissoluble and changeable, each of the two terms being also its opposite and complementary term. This is expressed by the traditional figure:

At the moment when the Yang (white, active) is at its apogee — the bulging, enlarged part — the Yin (black, passive) imperceptibly takes its place — the tapering part — and vice versa.

The Yin and the Yang have no 'moral' character, neither is superior nor inferior to the other. Their antithesis is as necessary and as little in conflict as that of the left hand and the right hand striking together to applaud.

17

THE YIN AND THE YANG TYPES

The Rat, Ox, Rabbit, Monkey, Dog and Pig are **Yin**.
The Tiger, Horse, Dragon, Snake, Goat and Rooster are
Yang.

The Yin man
Appearance: The Yin man is often corpulent, of medium
height and muscularly well developed. He is physically
resilient to a marked degree and his health is sound. He
often has a round face and does not smile much.
Psychology: The Yin man is above all self-preoccupied and
inclined to consider himself the centre of the universe.
Though his behaviour appears calm, his moods are unstable
and susceptible to his immediate environment. He has great
confidence in himself, yet fears failure. Sociable, hospitable,
he is optimistic vis-à-vis himself and others. His life is active;
he is pragmatic and efficient.

The Yang man
Appearance: He is of average weight, often tall and slender,
even willowy. His face is smiling and he prefers strong
colours. Of delicate health, he should be advised to prevent
rather than wait to cure illness.
Psychology: The Yang man is an individualist and attracted
to introspective meditation. He is intelligent, independent
and at times solitary. He prefers his own company and
communing with nature to living with the crowd. Contrary
to the Yin man, he seeks his equilibrium within himself
instead of finding it amongst others.

THE DOMAINS OF THE SNAKE

十二生肖

THE SNAKE AND ITS SYMBOLISM

The Snake, lord of the tortuous, silent and sinuous, has haunted our dreams and legends since the beginning of time, exciting in turn our anxieties and desires, attracting and repulsing. Whether coiled beneath a stone, winding round our hearts or poised with head high before our astounded eyes, the Snake is always present. Companion of sorcerers and seers, his symbol is the circle — one of the highest because it pertains to the infinite and thus to all esoteric knowledge. In the East, in tantric Yoga and Buddhism, he incarnates the *Kundalini*, those essential and subtle energies that circulate from the base of the spine to the top of the skull, connecting vital mental and suprapsychic spheres. The awakening and liberation of the *Kundalini Snake* constitutes one of the decisive steps towards spiritual discovery, arousing formidable paranormal powers, such as telepathy, clairvoyance and levitation.

The Snake recalls us continuously to his multiple universes, symbols and myths, ceaselessly astonishing and surprising us, even in our sleep. Sacred reptile? Or representative of evil, demon and god of Mother Earth, inhabiting at will waters, marshlands, mud and peat bogs? Crawling from the depths of the earth, emanating from chaos, he rises from the mists of time and from the most obscure depths of our unconscious, which he has always nourished with dreams and illusions.

The Snake's image is inseparable from Chinese culture and civilization, for he is the mythical father of the Chinese emperors. His legend is as follows:

In the beginning was chaos; only animal life existed. Somewhere between the heavens and the earth lay a life composed of forms and matter, replete with marvellous colours, divine sounds and intoxicating perfumes. But no being could perceive these colours, smell these perfumes or hear these sounds.

Fire heated the shell of chaos, licking its enormous egg with thousands of flames, diffusing its creative heat, watching over its hearth, its 'cauldron', its life. All that belonged to lightness formed the sky and all that belonged to heaviness formed the earth.

And then Pan-Ku was born and the organization of the world began. Pan-Ku grew up to become the Great All: he joined the heavens with the earth, his skull touched the summit, the starry vault; his body pierced the heavens and his feet dug deep into Mother-Earth.

The years passed. The sky became higher, the earth heavier and increasingly unfathomable. Pan-Ku created the wind, space and clouds; he caused thunder and lightning to rumble and flash. To heat the earth, he gave the sun; to create cold, he offered the moon. Finally, Pan-Ku gave his own blood, body-fluids, skin and hair. And, with a last kiss, he abandoned his teeth and bones to become stones and metals to solidify the earth.

Through Pan-Ku the sun heated the earth, the moon shone and the planets and stars were born. But until the arrival of Nu-Wa, no human being had appeared. Nu-Wa's beauty was incomparable, his virtues those of the wise. His body was that of a snake and his head of a human being.

Crawling on the earth, Nu-Wa became intoxicated with the thousands of perfumes emanating from it and understood that they were the aroma of life. Using his mouth to dig into the yellow earth, he heaped it up and moulded it for a long time. Thus a human being came into the world from the mouth of Nu-Wa, possessing the head of a man and the body of a monkey. This was the ancestor of the first emperors of China.

A few notes on the Snake
Principal qualities: Reflective, organized, alert and wise.
Principal defects: Jealous and obstinate. Does not listen to a word one says to him.

Work: Wilful, determined. Believes in physical and mental economy, organizing and calculating his actions without any waste of effort and energy.

Best role: Professor of philosophy. He adores Greek and Latin.

Worst role: Assembly-line worker; it would literally make him ill.

Money: Ambiguous. Not very economical, although circumspect. Likes to please himself and lives from day to day, counting on luck, chance and his intelligence.

Luck: To be born on a warm summer day. A Snake born in winter on a stormy night will be in danger all his life.

Cannot live without: Pleasing others.

Adores: Ornamentation and long nightly confidences in bed.

Detests: To be taken in or set up as an example.

Leisure activities: He likes to repaint the walls, change his possessions round and spend tranquil weekends in the country playing classical music and reading.

Favourite places: The desert; dry, wild stretches of land under a limpid sky — and his own home.

Colours: Red and green.

Plants: A rock-garden, ferns.

Flowers: Heather, thistle.

Professions: Professor, philosopher, teacher, psychiatrist, psychologist, diplomat, ambassador, astrologer, clairvoyant, head of personnel — and all professions requiring the skill of divination.

The four ages in the life of the Snake according to Chinese tradition

The *childhood* of the Snake will be happy, but only if calmness reigns within his family, otherwise this age will be critical. His *youth* will be free of problems. On the other hand, in *maturity* he will be at the mercy of all kinds of passions and his emotional life will often be unstable. In *old age* he will finally profit from his wisdom, although the fires of love will die slowly and are likely to cause him problems for a long time.

THE PSYCHOLOGY OF THE SNAKE

There are few animals in the world as rich in symbolic significance as the Snake; an entire book would hardly suffice to enumerate them. From the snake who bites his tail, symbol of eternal renewal, to the snake of the Tibetan 'Book of the Dead' ('I am the Snake Sata who lives in the furtherest reaches of the earth. I die, I am reborn, I am renewed and I become young each day . . .'), to China where he represents wisdom, this crawling creature accumulates dreams and nightmares and serves as an outlet for a plentitude of anxieties. Who does not recoil before a snake? Even when one knows very well it is not poisonous, our initial reaction is one of fear or disgust. If its bite represents a danger — and in some countries a mortal one — our terror knows no limits.

However, if we made the effort to overcome our prejudices, we might admit that, on a strictly aesthetic level, a snake is beautiful. Supple, sinuous and glossy, he fascinates, strangles, poisons or paralyses. He is endowed with an infinity of quasi-magical powers.

The snake of our earliest childhood memories is the one that caused such disorder in God's earthy paradise. No wonder he is feared! We tend to forget that he was only a vehicle adopted by Satan to lead Eve into temptation, an appearance on which our judgement has been based for generations. What a heavy heritage for these poor creatures who certainly never asked for it!

This analogy with sacred history is what brings us closest to the Snake as a sign of the Chinese zodiac. In the zodiac, as in the Bible, he is the *tempter* — the most seductive, fascinating and, in one sense, the most dangerous. Chinese astrological tradition affirms that no other signs, except those of the Tiger, Monkey, and sometimes the Pig, can resist his charm — a natural quality of persons born during the years of the Snake. These creatures are endowed with a kind of inner radiance which has nothing in common with, for example, the sparkling brilliance of the Dragon, but which radiates, charms and wins over the most forbidding and sceptical of individuals.

Those born under the sign of the Snake are distinguished, polished and elegant, refined in their dress and bearing. Handsome or ugly, they all have 'something' which attracts from the start because they are amiable, sociable and polite. In social gatherings they attract attention by their humour and the brilliance of their conversation, and they hold this attention because one senses that underneath this agreeable appearance lies a mystery and depth which is absolutely fascinating. It is this harmonious relationship between a well-prepared, polished exterior and a reflective, lucid personality which makes Snakes irresistible. And they know it, paying attention to both sides, caressing one and cultivating the other.

Endowed with a power of rapid intellectual assimilation, they are constantly learning something new; characteristic-ally, they adore reading and are real library-mice. They use their knowledge to charm their audience and derive great satisfaction from doing so, for they need to exchange ideas and debate opinions. Dialogue is as indispensable to them as the air they breathe. But the dialogue must not be superficial, but rather philosophic and even abstract. Snakes are known to spend entire nights in long intellectual discussions punctuated by reflective silences when one of them pronounces a 'historic phrase' or discovers another way to remodel the world. Conversation with Snakes is always agreeable, for they are profound, intelligent, thoughtful and cultivated, and possess wise answers to many questions. Their judgement, generally free from prejudice, is based on observation. They dislike disputes, violence and vulgarity; loud people who lose control of themselves literally make them squirm, and they will glide rapidly away from them, hissing as they go. They tolerate only music and sotto-voce conversations. I almost forgot: Snakes also love applause — but only when they have earned it and are feeling proud of themselves.

Snakes are intuitive; one can even speak of a 'sixth sense'. They instinctively feel things before they occur and detect the inner thoughts of others when conversing. All this, along with their imagination and mental alertness, makes them well-armed for the battle of life.

Their behaviour is calm and peaceful, for they love harmony and stability. They are also adaptable, well-balanced and endowed with a firm will which they reveal without hesitation when their moral or material comfort is threatened, reacting with the same vindictive vivacity as does their animal sign when someone steps on its tail. The rest of the time they doze. Snakes believe in making the least possible effort: if they can do their work correctly in an hour, they feel there is no point in working longer. The time thus gained will be spent reading a book in a comfortable armchair or stretched out on a soft carpet. When Snakes have nothing to do they can be amazingly lazy. They will yawn, roam around in a state of semi-undress, arrange flowers, water the plants, listen to music and move objects around. Then they will fall asleep, waking very late in the morning.

On the other hand, if they really wish to obtain something they are capable of moving heaven and earth to achieve their ends, even going so far as to discreetly eliminate their competitors. When the motive is strong enough, they are extremely persevering.

Snakes are lucky and, happily for them, often win their battles, for they are bad losers. They take failure as a personal affront and do not tolerate insults.

They are good advisors, understanding and far-sighted, who like to help their friends — as long as money is not involved, for they are quite stingy. But they adore being asked for help.

However, Snakes do have some defects: they do not listen to a word of what is said to them. Nor do they listen to advice, or, if they do, they assimilate it and a year later announce it as their own. They are capable of lying if the 'circumstances' and their wellbeing demand it. Very vulnerable, they detest being put in the wrong, contradicted or criticized, which brings out their aggressive instincts. They then become unkind — even hypocritical and vindicative — and seek revenge, which they will pursue for a long time.

THE SNAKE AS A CHILD

The child born during a year of the Snake is not difficult to raise because his need for peace and tranquillity is such that from his earliest years he will make the effort to adapt to personalities very different from his own. Also, he spontaneously seeks to please and understand his parents and loves to be treated as an adult. He appreciates being told secrets (a proof of confidence in him which reassures him) and does not fear responsibilities.

On the other hand, the Snake child has an enormous need for affection and tenderness; the slightest sign of interest in someone else can make him anxious and demoralize him. Consequently, if you desire a Snake child, remember first of all that he needs to be *preferred*. Extremely exclusive, he would not tolerate sharing his parents' love with a swarm of brothers and sisters: he should be an only child, around whose cradle the good fairies assemble with a chorus of fond and admiring exclamations.

One might well think that if the Snake child were made to share he would become less exclusive and demanding. Perhaps, but more likely this would only arouse a host of anxieties in him for which he would compensate by developing the defects of his sign, becoming introverted, vindictive or even sly. Extremely attached to his parents, the Snake child is sensitive to family harmony. Parental disputes risk scarring him forever, just as the shortest absence is felt to be a painful abandonment. However, if his parents should divorce he will be happier staying with one of them rather than being torn between the two. But the parent in question should be prepared for some problems if he or she should decide to remarry; the step-parent will need a great deal of diplomacy when dealing with the little Snake.

The young Snake works well at school, but erratically: zero in some subjects, brilliant in others. He is often gifted for artistic pursuits and literature. He does not enjoy violent games, preferring creative activities. Irregular in his work rhythm, he needs a lot of rest and relaxation.

LOVE LIFE

The Snake is one of the most seductive signs of the Chinese zodiac. According to tradition, the other animals are advised to flee from the Snake for they cannot resist him.

Why does the Snake have such a dangerous reputation? Because, it is said, he spends an enormous amount of energy seducing his victims, whom he then coils round and stifles. Once his prey has consented and been carefully immobilized, the Snake will seek another adventure, frequenting night haunts in search of his next victim.

Let us try to understand a little better why this is. Snakes are exclusive and jealous people; they love to feel they are the centre of the universe in their partner's eyes. Although they may accept that their spouse is interested in his work (one must, after all, live, and the Snake is realistic), once they believe that their partner has found some greater interest or more stimulating dialogue, they will be dramatically wounded; it will be unpardonable. To the Snake, the best means of avoiding such disquiet and anxiety is to immobilize his or her partner.

Fidelity is another question. Snakes have a very individual conception of it, and the male above all, who believes he is being perfectly faithful if he returns home regularly. The female Snake is more stable, but detests feeling cornered and prefers to retain a minimum of liberty and independence.

Both sexes have a profound need to please and attract, which gives them the impression that they truly exist. It is natural for them to behave charmingly, but this must not be taken advantage of; if they are the victims of a jealous scene they will become even more distant and move even further away.

Snakes are sensual, passionate, and blossom in a relationship based as much on physical compatibility as on dialogue. Even so, good communication with their partner is absolutely indispensable. They love to exchange ideas about books, music or unusual philosophical problems. When Snakes find what they have been seeking, they are easy to live with and are tolerant, understanding and conciliatory. But they will always have a vague idea of possession in the back of their minds — sometimes in spite of themselves.

FAMILY LIFE

If the male Snake does not always have an excellent reputation in Far Eastern countries (he is considered to be a Don Juan and seducer; inconstant, but charming), the female is sought for in marriage, being often beautiful, usually wise and always an excellent housekeeper. Both sexes are faithful to their families and, even when they stretch the marriage contract a bit, their fear of violent ruptures causes them to return regularly to the conjugal home. The fact that they are understanding parents sometimes undermines their authority, for 'putting themselves in their children's place', they find they are unable to direct them objectively.

Children born under the sign of the Rat, Dragon or Rooster will get along very well with a father or mother Snake, who in turn will be amused by them. Young Goats and Pigs will be a bit too much under the thumb of their Snake parents, who should encourage them to leave the family nest, however great the effort. A Snake parent will have great difficulty coping with the obstinate character of an Ox child, the independence of a Tiger or a Horse, or the passionate idealism of a Dog; these children will find their parents difficult. With a Monkey child, the relationship will be based more on comradeship than authority, and both will be very happy together. The Rabbit child will feel secure. But if an adult Snake has a child born in his own sign, he will smother it, and the young Snake will suffer acutely in cutting the umbilical cord.

As a rule, Snakes are comfortable in a married state, provided they are given minimal liberty; the legal bond reassures them and allows them the better to possess their partner. But if their choice is not a wise one, they will be exposed to the dangers of adultery and hidden passions. They should therefore reflect carefully before committing themselves, for the slightest error will lead them towards an exceedingly unstable emotional life — the opposite of what they need. They will do better to marry late when they have had some solid experience.

PROFESSIONAL LIFE

Those born under the sign of the Snake have mixed views about success. One has to remember that their principal quality — wisdom — distances them considerably from conflicts, rivalries and other such power struggles. The Snake's ambition can be defined in a single phrase: 'to be able to lead the life I like'. If he is near the point of success he will be remorseless, laying traps for his adversaries and revealing himself to be calculating, canny and even hypocritical. When he has attained his goal he will calm down, often perfectly content to enjoy his acquisitions voluptuously. He will feel no need to go any further, to make enemies or to become a victim of over-work for the sake of additional wealth or power.

Naturally, the Snakes' need for quality prohibits them from attaining the easier satisfactions of life. This is why they continue to struggle on mechanically, never over-tiring themselves. Also, success suits them: they know very well how to use their charm and are masters at insinuating themselves into the good graces of their superiors until they have become indispensable to them. Without getting into trouble, they fulfill marvellously the delicate tasks of mediator, intermediary and public relations. They know how to present an idea and how to outline a programme logically and coolly. When not using their charm, Snakes will keep it in reserve — and put forth another quality: their sense of organization.

If they want to, they can carry out a difficult job without appearing overworked yet without letting others overlook their merit in doing so. They are intelligent, determined and courageous people, and very conscious of their potential. But sometimes, due to their laziness, they will leave it to others to act — and even work — in their place. In the last lap of certain triumph, they will take up the torch; but they will be yawning. The Snake is the most opportunistic of all the Chinese signs: he will know how to seize any valuable opportunity and leave aside those with lesser attractions. He will even go so far as to help you — if you can be of use to him. If this fails, he will try something else. He is never finished with experiences.

MATERIAL LIFE

Snakes love money because it gives them the lifestyle they want: surrounding themselves with pretty objects, holidaying on tropical beaches, buying new clothes regularly and all the books and records they might wish. Without money, they would not be able to do this, and they know it. 'I must have' is their motto. And when a Snake has decided that he needs something, he gets it! They are not at all ashamed to admit this. After all, is it not natural to seek what one desires? Even the idealistic Dog has no answer to that question.

Thus Snakes are self-seeking. They are not the kind to fall in love before investigating their partner's bank account. They accept that they would never have the same tastes as a hippy in ragged blue jeans — unless he or she was the son or daughter of a Greek shipowner. If someone proposes a job, they immediately make inquiries about its financial potential. Snakes have no false modesty.

Being lucky and resolute social climbers, they can be counted on to achieve a certain affluence in their life style; they rarely lack money.

Snakes are not lenders; 'charity begins at home' is another of their mottos. But they are not economical either and spend what they have rapidly for their pleasure and well-being. Unlike Tigers, Snakes do not like to take risks; they are not speculators. As long as they do not have to deprive themselves of anything, their interest in the material side of life will be satisfied; not because they have money put aside, but because they count on luck and destiny to put them in the path of new funds. Nevertheless, Snakes do hanker after a little security, a few investments they can count on. When they are in love or wish to seduce someone, they will find presents enough; and they spoil their family, but only when the mood strikes them.

ENVIRONMENT

The French poet Baudelaire wrote of beds full of gentle aromas, divans deep as tombs and strange flowers adorning rooms. Himself a Snake, the poet's vision is representative of the universe of this sign. Snakes are people of refinement who adore ancient objects, inlaid furniture and delicately coloured Persian carpets — preferably a little worn. Their taste is faultless: they understand the harmony of colour and shape. Their equilibrium requires that they live in an environment they have created in their own image: if you enter a Snake's home you will see immediately whether it was he who chose the decoration because it will *resemble him*. If not, you can be sure that he will soon move — or redecorate the entire place.

Everything in a Snake's home is definitely comfortable and designed for the pleasure of the senses. It is as though our Snake counted on his home to complete his conquests of the outside world, with classical music playing softly, deep cushions, perfumed candles, lovely flowers, a well-filled library and rare liqueurs and wines.

Naturally, there is the other side of the coin: some cupboards will be in disarray, and he will pass systematically behind you to empty the ashtrays and replace objects that you may have moved by only an inch. He does not do this to vex you; it is a mechanical reaction.

Wherever he goes, the Snake will repaint the walls; he would be a nervous wreck if he had to live with someone else's colour scheme. He detests hotels, anywhere temporary and all furnished places. He often carries with him a pile of ravishing but useless knick-knacks which help him to recreate his personal universe.

It is difficult for him to live with someone because he cannot adapt to tastes other than his own. Environment is perhaps the one area in which he is the least compromising. Male or female, the Snake always needs his own little bachelor flat, office or room. His well-being depends on it.

A guide to personal relations with a Snake

Methods of seduction: Indescribable. A knowing mixture of detached charm, sensuality, niceness and understanding — all blended differently depending on the Snake, but with the ingredients always the same. And then, to all this physical seduction (they are handsome!), one must add their innate fascination and magic, their astonishing ability to persuade others.

If he loves you: Immediately resist him (he hates it!), for tomorrow it will be too late. He does not need much time to make himself indispensable. If you love him too — good luck! Try to maintain a minimum of independence: he will complain, but will respect you all the more for it; and the respect of a Snake is precious.

He expects of you: That you be unconditionally faithful.

To keep you: He will find your weak point — the chink in your armour — and will use it to soften your heart, to exalt you, listen to you — which he knows so well how to do!

If he is unfaithful: It is for the sheer pleasure of doing so, to be able to murmur under his breath, 'Ah, now I have the better of you!'

If you are unfaithful: He will be deeply shocked. If he loves you a great deal he will try to understand, but it will be difficult for him.

In case of a break between you: If you succeed in getting rid of him, congratulations — you deserve a medal. He will resort to any means to avoid being abandoned, which he hates. He also does not like to initiate the break, unless he wishes to teach you a lesson.

If you wish to give him a gift: It will cost a lot. Offer Mr Snake a work of art or a rare book, or a complete collection of classical records and tapes. Offer Mrs Snake a discreet jewel, but make sure it is real, for Snakes detest fakes and will be contemptuous if you offer one to them.

If you want to seduce him: Make him spend a sleepless night of mad caresses and intimate secrets. But rest up well beforehand.

If you want to get rid of him: Invite him to spend a weekend at your home. Without warning him that another admirer is in the bath, ask him if he wants to freshen up.

THE SNAKE AND THE OTHER CHINESE SIGNS

Snake/Rat

This is a strange mixture. At first glance both appear calm, clever and opportunistic, which makes for a positive common ground, above all in the field of business. But the Rat is active, and the Snake prefers a minimum of effort. The one will shake up the other, who in turn will calm him. Both are possessive, and the Snake has a completely relative notion of fidelity. If unfaithful to his partner, the Snake will only grudgingly accept that his partner is likely to do the same. The Rat will unsheathe his claws, the Snake will try to smother him. Life will become increasingly complicated.

In fact, the Rat and Snake do not need each other, for they are capable, as the occasion requires, of using the same weapons with equal efficiency. But as comrades they respect each other, and, sharing a taste for black humour, have fun together. If they establish an emotional tie, it will depend on mutual tolerance, a quality not notable in either. However, that is the only way they will be able to get along together. Generally speaking, they understand each other, and the Snake's quiet smile always calms the Rat's aggressiveness. But beware: such complicity is deep and secret; only they can sustain it.

Snake/Ox

A little good will on both sides will suffice, for the Snake gets along with almost everyone. The Ox will think that it is he who dominates, which will please him; and his Snake spouse, a willing believer in the less effort the better, will certainly not discourage him. She will surround and net him, as much by understanding as by complimenting him on his seriousness and his sense of responsibility, coiling about him with delight. The Snake, who loves comfort, does not lack will; but if he finds someone ready to work for two, he will only do what is strictly necessary — and then only to keep up appearances. And so the Ox will be consumed but remain content, and the Snake will also be content, feeling secure. Reassured of the fidelity of his companion, the Snake will indulge in a few discreet extras for amusement, but no-one will know about them.

On a business level, they compliment each other; one will work while the other reflects. Together they will be able to amass a considerable fortune.

Snake/Tiger

Hardly advisable. The vitality of the Tiger is likely to be too much for the contemplative Snake, who will neither wish nor be able to follow the busy, bustling rhythm that his companion imposes on his entourage.

Although peaceful, reflective and sometimes lazy, the Snake does not need to be aroused from his natural rhythm. He is capable of managing quite effectively in his own way and hates to be given advice. Sometimes dogmatic, which no Tiger can tolerate, he is possessive and tortuous, preferring the curved line to the straight, if by this he achieves his objective. In short, the Snake thinks of the end, while the Tiger relishes the means, hoping it to be admirable and delightful. They do not really understand each other and will often avoid each other. The Tiger will distrust the Snake's meanderings, and the Snake will be intelligent enough to avoid the Tiger, realizing that such an animal cannot be possessed.

On the other hand, this could be a marvellous business alliance. They complement each other beautifully, with one taking the risks and the other calculating behind the scenes. But they should not live together, for the Snake would betray the Tiger, who would in turn certainly destroy him.

Snake/Rabbit
They have in common a love of peace, security and aesthetic taste. They will tend to give preference to their home, environment and comfort and will appreciate beautiful objects and places. They would make a good pair of decorators. To have peace the Rabbit will have the wisdom to let the Snake think that he is the boss and master — at least on the emotional level. But the Rabbit's hesitations, and above all his virtuous side, will annoy the Snake whose sense of values is much more elastic.

However, whether it be love or friendship, this tie will be profitable for both. With patience, the Rabbit will perhaps succeed in persuading the Snake to accept another's opinion; and the Snake, who does not fear danger and adapts to all situations, will teach the Rabbit to be more philosophic.

Snake/Dragon
Traditionally this is one of the best friendly alliances for the

Dragon — especially when the Snake is the female. Although he must feel he is the stronger, the male Dragon needs to be proud of his wife; and female Snakes are wise, seductive and elegant. Nor will any female Snake be stupid enough to make her power apparent; the 'underground' manoeuvre is much more to her nature.

If the Dragon is female, the relationship will be more delicate: she will hope to be adulated by her Snake husband, a hope which he will satisfy for a while out of kindness, nevertheless coiling round her like a boa constrictor. Unfortunately, female Dragons dislike feeling smothered.

However, despite the Dragon's need to 'shine at any price', and the possessiveness of the Snake, this relationship is to be recommended. These Chinese zodiacal neighbours respect and rarely deceive each other: the Dragon has too much honour to wish to be diminished in someone's estimation, and the Snake is tolerant enough to withhold his criticisms concerning the flames and turbulence of his partner.

Snake/Snake

In friendship and in work Snakes appreciate the value of each other. Wearing a sly smile, they will amuse themselves by playing tricks on each other and setting traps for the sole pleasure of seeing the other escape. They will make each other laugh and have a lovely time together. But only in small doses. Chinese astrology is strict on one point: two Snakes cannot live together because they will stifle each other. This is true of all relationships between Snakes, particularly when in love or between parents and children. When these delicious reptiles live too close to one another they fade, as when one snuffs out a candle. And, since they are aware of this and since their discretion is nowhere near great enough to persuade them to take a back-seat, they become furious.

If you are a Snake who loves another Snake, do not live together. Meet from time to time, but if it is more than once a week, you might be in trouble!

Snake/Horse

The Horse will often be seduced by the Snake, and will remain almost faithful to him. He will have the impression — extremely mistaken — of being as free as the air; in fact, his Snake companion, coiled up in a corner of his imaginative brain, will be ceaselessly present and indispensable. On his side, the philosophic Snake will not take offence at being regarded occasionally as a piece of furniture, and will know how to find his own interests. The Horse will amuse him by his shifts in mood and he will have the impression of being at the circus.

But the day will come when the Horse's egotism will cause him to tire of his Snake companion, who will have trouble replacing him. This will not be bad for the Horse: it will allow him to avoid being swallowed up.

Still, this relationship is positive and exalting, especially at the start when the Horse is still blinded by passion and if there is some external obstacle to be overcome. If there is none in sight, they will have no trouble inventing one.

Snake/Goat

There is no problem with their getting along with each other. The Snake infinitely appreciates the fantasy, imagination and creativity of the Goat, and a love of art, beauty and harmony often unites them. And, they will rarely quarrel as it is too tiring.

But which of the two will do the work? On this level, the Goat is irregular and rather badly organized, and the Snake cannot be counted on to keep the accounts. And, when the Goat works and earns money, he wants it for himself — 'me first' — and perhaps a small gift from time to time as well.

If they have inherited some property they will live together peaceably, from time to time doing a little work, not so much to earn money as for the pleasure of it and to prove to others that they can do it. They will pitilessly mock commuters, those victims of the train-desk-sleep syndrome. They will wallow in their respective egotisms, and, even if the Goat occasionally strains on his leash, the relationship will work out in the end; bitterness and divorce are too fatiguing.

Snake/Monkey
Here there will be intellectual compatibility because, on this level, the Snake and Monkey are the most 'endowed' of the Chinese zodiac. They assimilate easily and think fast and effortlessly, adapting themselves to just about everything.

They complete each other: the Monkey is the cleverer on the surface, the Snake in depth. They would make an excellent business team, crammed with ideas and possibilities. They should not hesitate to join forces.

But emotionally, it is another story. The Monkey is traditionally one of the few signs capable of eluding the Snake's grasp. He will not allow himself to be eaten up, and the Snake, disgusted, will not persevere for long but will look for more acquiescent prey. Their reciprocal fidelity would not last for long. They should remain friends — easier and more profitable.

Snake/Rooster
This is the ideal couple of Chinese astrology. Traditionally they represent mind and matter, balancing themselves in harmonious union. They get along marvellously together. From the start they will appreciate each other's elegance: they could even buy matching outfits and look like fashion photographs. They love each other for their flattering appearance as a couple; even more, they understand each other perfectly. The Rooster will be able to sing in peace, and, between cock-a-doodle-do's, will recount his exploits to the Snake, who will comment on them with wit and humour. The Snake will feel secure because of the hard-

working side of the farm-yard king, who will finally feel understood, being accepted as he is and not judged only by his brilliant plumage.

The Rooster and the Snake are accomplices. Even if they argue — usually because of an infidelity — their dialogue will always bring them together; they adore philosophizing into the small hours of the morning.

Snake/Dog

In general, Dogs like Snakes very much. They appreciate their wisdom and depth and forget their selfish and ambitious sides. They idealize them willingly, for the Snake's capacity for reflection makes them feel secure. One may well ask why, but that is simply the way it is.

Snakes, on the other hand, sincerely admire the honesty of Dogs, even if they are not disposed to imitate them. As a couple it can work out rather well, as long as the Snake accepts being idealized. But this will not satisfy him for long, because in matters of love he likes difficulty. So, as time goes by, he will glide around all over the place, having completely immobilized his Dog spouse, who will be left in charge of everything. The Dog, however, will remain content, for her Snake will return regularly to coil round her to keep her dependent. With the help of love from one and tenderness from the other, they will go far and be happy. Who are we to complain?

Snake/Pig

Not an obvious alliance. From the start, the Pig runs the risk of being completely taken in by the Snake, whose honesty is relative and highly personal. The unaffected nature of the Pig will often annoy the Snake, who will judge it — sometimes wrongly, but not always — as credulity, even innocence. After all, who would not raise his eyebrows when a Pig lets himself go with some lightly risque remarks?

Despite these difficulties, their powerful sensuality will unite them — even if it is not expressed in the same way.

The Snake, in any case, will eat the Pig in choice morsels. But here comes the surprise: the Pig will react quickly and will know how to extricate himself from the Snake's coils. Like the Monkey and the Tiger, he is capable of resisting the Snake, although not without leaving some skin behind. He should therefore be careful before allowing himself to be buried in the coils of this dangerous reptile; and the Snake should not mistake the Pig for a toy, or he will be in for some unpleasant surprises.

SOME SNAKE CELEBRITIES

Baden-Powell, Bela Bartok, Baudelaire, Borodin, Brahms, Louis Braille, Calvin, Copernicus, Darwin, Dostoyevsky, Flaubert, Faure, Arthur Fleming, Henry Fonda, Gandhi, Garbo, Paul Getty, Andre Gide, Gladstone, Goethe, Gogol, Princess Grace, John Kennedy, Landru, Lincoln, Harold Lloyd, Louis-Philippe, Martin Luther King, Mao Tse-tung, Madame Mao, Matisse, Mendelssohn, Miro, Montaigne, Montesquieu, Nobel, Jacqueline Onassis, Picasso, Edgar Allan Poe, Richelieu, Sartre, Schubert, Tennyson, St Vincent of Paul, Mae West.

YOUR
COMPANION
IN LIFE

生命伴侶

After the Chinese sign of your year of birth, here is the sign of your hour of birth

What is a Companion in Life, as understood in Chinese astrology? It is a sort of 'ascendant' sign corresponding to your hour of birth. This Companion is another animal belonging to the Chinese cycle of the twelve emblematic beasts, who falls into step with you and accompanies you, ever ready to help you brave the traps and ambushes along your route. A permanent and benevolent shadow, he can render the impossible possible.

He is your counterpart, but with his own character and tendencies and with a different psychology. Both guardian angel and devil's advocate, he will be a witness to your life and an actor in it.

Have you ever felt, deep inside yourself, the subtle presence of another 'myself' inhabiting you and with whom you live, at times in harmony, at others in conflict? Another self who sometimes criticizes you and at others encourages you? That is your Companion in Life.

There are times when he will appear to be an imposter or an intruder. Certainly, he often questions your habits and your moral or spiritual complacency. Accompanied by this companion, a shadow within, the route is less monotonous and the voyager multiplies his chances of arriving at his chosen destination. This, however, in itself matters little, for it is the journey and the manner in which it is conducted that are important. Indolence is the greatest danger: your Companion is capable of arousing you from a lassitude of spirit and, to that end, if necessary, robbing you of your certainties, trampling on your secret gardens and, finally, tearing away the great veil of illusion.

It sometimes happens that your Companion is of the same sign as your year of birth, a twin brother in a way — for example, a Snake/Snake. In this case, you must recognize that he will compel you to realize yourself fully and to live the double aspect — the Yin and the Yang — that your bear within yourself. In any case, you also bear within yourself the twelve animals. So, set out on the long route, ready for the great adventure: the beautiful voyage during which you will encounter the harmoniously entangled, the solemn and the grotesque, the ephemeral reality, the dream and the imagined.

Table of hours corresponding to the twelve emblematic animals

If you were **born** between	11 pm and 1 am	your **companion** is	Rat
	1 am and 3 am		Ox
	3 am and 5 am		Tiger
	5 am and 7 am		Rabbit
	7 am and 9 am		Dragon
	9 am and 11 am		Snake
	11 am and 1 pm		Horse
	1 pm and 3 pm		Goat
	3 pm and 5 pm		Monkey
	5 pm and 7 pm		Rooster
	7 pm and 9 pm		Dog
	9 pm and 11 pm		Pig

These figures correspond to the *solar hour* of your birth. If necessary, you should check the summer times (Daylight Savings Time) and make the appropriate adjustment (sometimes two hours before or after statutory time).

THE SNAKE AND ITS COMPANION IN LIFE

Snake/Rat

These two are brothers, but they fight each other mercilessly. Their territory is identical, but they have won it with bites and scratches, venom and trickery. The Rat and Snake are masters of the art of attack; moreover they are intuitive, professional spellbinders, who run the risk of putting each other to sleep by using mutual hypnosis. Alas, in this situation, the Rat cannot reverse roles.

The Snake will not lend himself to this little game. For the Rat the Snake Companion will always remain a mysterious reptile, coiled up under a stone, waiting to drag him at times into perilous labyrinths.

Snake/Ox

The Ox will often be disorientated by the aggressiveness of his Snake Companion, who can nurture a dormant capacity for violence in him. The peaceful Ox, his eyes fixed on the blue line of the horizon, will not understand the behaviour of the reptile — his attacks, his secret hiding places, his sinuous approach. He will too often be tempted to crush him with a hoof, and in consequence will suffer many internal conflicts. The slow Ox, however, will be stimulated by this mysterious reptile who lures him to a fen and then shows him how he waits, hidden beneath a stone. Although his Serpent Companion disconcerts him, the Ox will certainly learn that there are paths that he must sometimes avoid.

Snake/Tiger

He is the professional charmer, crafty and sly if the need arises, capable of biting and releasing venom in order to attain his ends. However, moderation will win out over the ill-loved Snake's aggressiveness. Coiled within the Tiger, he can also be a welcome symbol of knowledge and of the underground world. Habituated to the honour due his rank, the Tiger is sometimes forgetful of those who crawl yet accomplish the same ends. The Snake who lies within may pretend humility; this is easy for him, since he is a prince of detours and winding paths. However, he should be careful not to fall into the traps he sets for others.

 Snake/Rabbit

A strange creature, whose head is not easily distinguished from its tail. In love with anything strange, but not an adventurer, the Snake/Rabbit will daydream about travelling while curled up in a soft armchair. 'Inhabited' by a price of wanderings, he has a taste for suspense, mystery and the subterranean, discovering hiding places buried under a stone. He will not hesitate to take on the colour of a wall for the pleasure of deceiving, surprising and disconcerting you. Elusive, clever and shifty, he is as dangerous as he is seductive. If you meet up with a Snake/Rabbit, pinch yourself, because he is a professional spell-binder. He will seduce you somehow — with his charm or by blackmail.

Snake/Dragon

A lucky and canny animal, the Snake/Dragon is a traveller on whom fortune will smile, and what he cannot obtain by force or charm he will obtain by malice and enchantment. If the Dragon sometimes makes the mistake of being too heavy or conventional, the Snake will lead him to value discretion, patience and the advantages of the indirect approach. A formidable beast, full of charm, he will bring a taste of mystery to his partner, who will shiver either with pleasure or with fear.

 Snake/Snake

Whether a rattlesnake, cobra or adder, he will prefer detours and by-ways to the main roads. But the result will be the same: he will arrive — slowly but surely — at the goal he has fixed for himself. The Snake/Snake will be unable to avoid complicating his life. When it seems too simple, he becomes bored; he always needs a little salt, a tasty sauce, because he is a complicated animal. Always on the defensive and slightly aggressive, he ardently cultivates a sense of property through his home which he makes a veritable refuge, an Ali-Baba cavern, piling up treasures which he jealously protects. If you sight him on your path, make a detour; even if you are not afraid of him, you reaction will give him so much pleasure!

Snake/Horse

He is a wise dandy, combining elegance and ardour with highly developed moral demands which can sometimes conflict with his pride. For the Snake/Horse is a bad loser and does not accept failure. He is a winner and will not hesitate to be opportunistic and sly, restraining neither his tongue nor his heart. Nevertheless, since he is irresistibly charming, the Snake/Horse will be excused for his boastfulness and even his ill-nature. But he should not overdo it!

 Snake/Goat

It will be rather dangerous to fall in love with him: it is impossible to expect fidelity from the Goat/Snake. This reptilian Goat is a fickle being charged with fantasy; an artist who will make a 'goat' of you if you try to seduce him. At first he will seem docile, seeking your protection: but he will then pull you joyously along by the tip of your nose. Exclusive and jealous, he is scarcely aware of the contradiction, for his own bad faith is disarming. In life he will enjoy plenty of good luck and have the advantage of good taste and a capacity for finesse; but his instability will cause him considerable damage, some of which he will not recover from, above all during his mature years.

Snake/Monkey

He will be rational and a good organizer, but he will not be able to conceal his strong superiority complex which, unless he takes care, will cause him major problems. An intelligent and quick animal, his tendency to get carried away will be tempered by deep reflection; even so, he will always refuse to listen to the advice of others, because of his pride and self-esteem. He will not entertain any argument about his ideas, still less that his work or his word be questioned. The Monkey/Snake is talkative, courageous and, at times, a liar. However, his ability and his subtlety are major trump cards.

Snake/Rooster

An intuitive and frank animal, he will accomplish his tasks with a generous heart and with much good will and honesty — thus correcting the Snake's tendency to side-track — which will not prevent him from being uneasy, despite his apparent self-assurance. The Snake/Rooster flares up easily, so be careful if it is one of his bad days. He will attack with surprising aggressiveness and be entirely unjust simply to reassure himself. Do not attempt to expose his faults with evidence; he will be narrow-minded and never forgive you for having discovered his weak points. The Snake/Rooster is overly concerned with projecting a good image. He has a need to shine and surround himself with costly and beautiful things; this may appear superficial, but it is vital for his morale.

Snake/Dog

He has a keen moral sense, is intuitive, but has a tendency to be pessimistic. Life with him can become very complicated. He is the kind to torment himself to excess, announcing the onset of a hurricane at the least rising of the wind, or a deluge after a few drops of rain. Ever on the watch and constantly on guard, he risks playing the role of the persecuted, one of those flayed alive, whose company one does not usually seek. This is a drawback, particularly since the Dog/Snake is courageous, warm and understands the meaning of faithfulness. However, he has a great need of love and reassurance.

 Snake/Pig

While he is peaceful, secretive and sensitive, he is also a bad loser and his motives are questionable. He does not like to lose and prefers solitude to risking failure. It is useless to try to distract him from his normal routine; he is too obstinate and distrustful. However, this does not stop him from being gullible. It is quite possible to 'take him in'; he will then oscillate between aggressiveness and running away, for at bottom he is tolerant but too proud to admit that his adversary may be right. Although he appears indifferent, the Snake/Pig actually loves money for its own sake and adores amassing treasures and booty. Apparently calm, deep within he is boiling. This solitary reptile is not lukewarm: he is a tough person with a tender heart.

THE SNAKE
AND THE FIVE
ELEMENTS

五行

YOUR ELEMENT

In Chinese astrology, each year is joined to an Element. There are five Elements: *Water, Fire, Wood, Metal, Earth.*

Each of the twelve emblematic animals is linked successively to each of the five Elements. For example, in the year 1900 the Rat was Earth, in 1912 he was Fire; in 1924 he was Metal, in 1936, Water and in 1948 he was Wood. Therefore, for the twelve years from 1900 he was linked to Earth, for the next twelve years to Fire, and, for every succeeding period of twelve years, to each of the other Elements, in succession.

In order to determine the Element corresponding to the year of your birth, use the table below:

> *Years whose digits end in:* 1 and 6 — Water
>
> 2 and 7 — Fire
>
> 3 and 8 — Wood
>
> 4 and 9 — Metal
>
> 5 and 0 — Earth

The same union of *Animal-Element* repeats every sixty years, for example, Rat-Earth appeared in 1720, 1780, 1840, 1900, 1960 and so on.

The five Elements are the primary forces affecting the universe. It is their particular association with each of the signs which provides the basis for every horoscope. Movement and fluctuation, Yin and Yang, these symbolic forces are in a perpetual state of action and interaction.

Wood gives birth to Fire, which gives birth to Earth, which gives birth to Metal, which gives birth to Water, which in turn gives birth to Wood.

SNAKE/WATER
(you were born in 1941)

The cold born of the northern sky descended to Earth and gave birth to Water. The Chinese consider Water more a synonym for coldness and ice than a symbol of fertility.

Characteristics of the Snake/Water

Water of winter nights, rigour and severity, calm and deep Water to be feared and respected, still Water sheltering underwater demons asleep in its depths; foetid and muddy Water of the marshes, a refuge of crawling creatures.

The Snake in love with humidity will be attracted to Water: marshes, ponds, stagnant pools, peat and bamboo. Such Water will not be bracing and invigorating for the Snake; it could provoke hesitation or even a halt in his sinuous course, a dangerous effect for this reptile with a Yang tendency, symbol of horizontal energy. The Snake/Water should therefore consider Water a passing Element only — a means or a tool, and not an end in itself.

Health of the Snake/Water

The Water organ is the kidney; its flavour is salty. Seek the bracing waters of the seaside, the torrents and the springs — but not mud baths, although they are excellent for rheumatism — and enjoy them in the sun, which is vital for you.

The Snake/Water and others

The Snake/Water will be calm and wise and his actions will be based on reflection. The Water Element will often be socially beneficial, calming the hyper-active side of the Snake, attracting him to meditation and the possibility of governing, mastery and control. The Snake/Water will then be just and honest; his words will carry weight and men will listen to him, allowing themselves to be guided by his wisdom and moderation. The Snake/Water will be non-violent, an enemy of anger, aggressiveness and uncontrolled force. He will be turned entirely towards his fellow men, intent on listening to their problems. An excellent psychologist or a prudent man of the law, he is a cool-headed leader and a warm, good-hearted man.

Advice for the Snake/Water
You have qualities which demand to be used, for the sake of others and for yourself; learn to discover them and put them into practice. Otherwise, they will turn against you, paralyse you and condemn you to be an eternal wanderer.

A Snake/Water year
The culminating point for a Snake/Water year will be winter, a period of gestation. The Yin of Water will balance the Yang of the Snake.

Profit from this year to restore your energies and regain your inner balance. You can be active, and successfully so, but avoid overwork and all excesses, which are so often followed by depression. Maintain your equilibrium and do not waste your energy, otherwise you will ruin everything by wanting to go too far too quickly.

Historical example of a Snake/Water year 1521

Francis I of France had not accepted the decision of the Electors whereby Charles V of Spain became the Holy Roman Emperor. He was to contest it until defeated at the battle of Pavia in 1525. The new Emperor had also to contend with a heresy which threatened to fracture the faith of Christendom.

Martin Luther preached that justification was not to be found by work or efforts of the will but through faith alone, the gift of God's grace. His notorious 95 theses aroused strong reactions, and not only in Germany: even Henry VIII of England wrote an anti-Lutheran tract for which he was awarded the title 'Defender of the Faith'.

When the Emperor summoned Luther to the Diet of Worms in 1521 he hoped to force him to recant. Equally Luther, who was nothing if not argumentative, was anxious to expound his views but required and obtained a safe conduct before he appeared. The assembly had no sympathy for his arguments; nor did they approve the manner of his journey. Clad as a monk he had been accompanied by a following fit for a count. At Erfurt and other cities he had preached before massed crowds, exuding physically the pugnacious cast of his mind. Nevertheless he was treated with consideration and allowed time for reflection when asked if he retracted the opinions expressed in his books. Fortified by the night, the solace of the mystic, he appeared the following day, resolute; he retracted nothing. He stood by what he had written.

Thus ended the confrontation at Worms and the unity of the Church. Even Henry VIII, Defender of the Faith, would shortly break with Rome.

SNAKE/WOOD
(you were born in 1953)

To the East the wind blew in the sky and from its warm caress of the Earth, Wood was born.

Characteristics of the Snake/Wood

Wood is of the morning and of springtime. Its temperate nature loves harmony, beauty and elegance. Springtime will be fertile for the Snake, bringing him equilibrium and a sense of creation, encouraging him to develop his taste and desire for harmony and beauty. Nature will become his ally and inspiration, a fountain to which the Snake will go to slake his thirst, to become stronger and to discover nature's multiple powers and secrets. But Wood also contains passion, anger and vulnerability which, if excessive, has a tendency to cause one to lose all sense of proportion and, in turn, become destructive and devastating. The Snake should remain vigilant and lucid and try not to give in to this negative aspect of his Element.

Health of the Snake/Wood

The organ of Wood is the liver; its flavour is acid. The Snake/Wood will be anxious and tormented. He will suffer from a psychosomatic illness and will often need to compensate by over-eating. Cakes and chocolates may then please him, but they will not please his liver.

The Snake/Wood and others

The Wood Element will have a positive influence on the Snake's social life. Aware of his weaknesses, such as his anxiety and self-questioning, he will respond to his predicament with a relaxed attitude, preferring his imagination to run free rather than be constricted by the rigid structures of a society in which he feels asphyxiated. This is a just and reasonable attitude especially suiting the Snake, who prefers the circle to the square and the curve to the angle. With deliberate improvisation, the Snake will extricate himself marvellously from the most difficult situations; he will glide and sneak in and out and let the storm pass; then, when it is all over, he will reappear, tranquil and calm. Inventive and creative, he will be a painter, poet, musician, craftsman, or even a gardener, nurseryman or landscape architect — someone who combines beauty with space.

Advice for a Snake/Wood

You are the symbol of harmony, charm and beauty; you dream of space and liberty. Relax and yield to the imaginative. You have the soul of an artist, so do not close yourself up in an office or allow yourself to be choked by conventional pursuits. Being of Wood, you would end up by drying up.

A Snake/Wood year

The culminating point for a Snake/Wood year will be spring,

a period of growth and prosperity. Beauty and harmony will be your companions during this year. The Snake/Wood will be in his best physical and mental form, supple and intuitive.

Historical example of a Snake/Wood year 1593

Henry of Navarre reverted to the Roman faith. Both the personal decision and its consequences were momentous. In an age when heresay amounted to treason against the state Henry, the legitimate heir to the last of the Valois, was also the avowed leader of the Huguenots, heretics, apostates and schismatics. France was riven by a civil war fired by religious dissension. The Catholic majority would never accept a Protestant as king, preferring to offer the throne to a Guise, even to the son of the Spanish King. The old furies roused by the presence of the infidel in Jerusalem were as nothing compared to the hatred for the schismatic in the sixteenth century. In England papacy was hated because of its threat by an alien authority. Over-governed since the days of Henry II the English temperament required the solitary reliefs afforded by the Protestant faith. The French sensed the need for control, both by their monarchy and the Church.

Henry, by his momentous decision, instinctively recognized this. He had tried but failed to subdue the capital. The resources of the Parisians were too strong for him, not only materially but spiritually; for the indulgent and complacent world of the Roman Church had risen with an iron will to combat the Protestant threat. Thus Henry determined on a policy of appeasement. He should be King of France first, secondly of the Faith, thirdly of that form of the Faith which appealed to his subjects.

On 23 July Henry publicly submitted to the authority of the Archbishop of Bourges and swore to defend the Catholic faith with his blood and his life and to die in it. He renounced the heresies of the schismatics of whom he had long been the leader. A week later he entered Paris, where he was accepted and welcomed as King.

SNAKE/FIRE
(you were born in 1917 or 1977)

Heat was born in the southern sky, descended to Earth and fertilized it. From their union, Fire was born.

Characteristics of the Snake/Fire
The Fire Element is of the midday, the South and summer. Fire is Yang; it is the Element which animates; it quickens and transforms.

The Fire that quickens the Snake will perpetually feed and renew his energy. But it could also become dangerous and destructive: A Fire which consumes and devours. The Snake/Fire must learn to control his Element. He must not let it go out or let it flare up, for then all would be consumed in its path.

The health of the Snake/Fire
The organ of Fire is the heart, its flavour is bitter. Fire of summer and southern climes: do not allow yourself to be carried away by anger and control your aggressiveness; all excessive outbursts entail a futile loss of energy. Overwork can lead to a heart attack; slow down and have regular medical checkups.

The Snake/Fire and others
Warrior Fire, but lucid and clairvoyant Fire, too. Passionate and violent Fire, preferring manoeuvres to diplomacy. The Snake/Fire will be a man of action and of war; an adventurer or an ardent political militant. He will often be a convinced and convincing individualist.

Alas, tolerance will not be his strong point; he will sometimes have to know how to throw water on his Fire, unless he is to end by mounting the pyre that he himself has lit.

Advice for a Snake/Fire
Take things upon yourself, but moderate your flame; you too easily set things ablaze and stir up discord which can turn against you.

A Snake/Fire year
The culminating point for a Snake/Fire year will be summer, a period of creation. Your Yang tendency will stretch toward the 'Great Yang', which will bring an unquenchable dynamism.

Historical example of a Snake/Fire year 1617

Both in England and in France the Monarch was ensnared. James I of England had been compelled to renounce his favourite, Robert Ker, who had accompanied him from Scotland as a page. By the time Ker was attainted and condemned he was the Earl of Somerset and the owner of Walter Raleigh's old manor at Sherborne in Dorset. George Villiers succeeded to the favours of the King. He had risen in much the same way as Ker, from page, cupbearer, gentleman of the bedchamber, to a knighthood, an estate and, in 1617, the Earldom of Buckingham. Buckingham flourished: Ker was to languish in prison until 1622.

The spice of pederasty was not the occasion of the French King's misfortune. He was the victim of his formidable mother, Marie de Medici, Regent of France, who had entrusted the affairs of the kingdom to one Concino Concini, an adventurer who required and was lavished with gifts and the peculations of office.

In 1617 Louis XIII officially came of age. But he was king in form only: the substance was denied him. Louis was not to be subborned. He made arrangements with his captain of the guard, Vitry. On the morning of 24 April Vitry and a group of courtiers stood about the entrance to the Louvre. Warned of Concini's approach he made to intercept him and announced to the astounded Florentine that he was under arrest. Concini, his hand to his sword, called for help but Vitry's accomplices were too quick for him. Five fired, one ball caught Concini between the eyes, one pierced an eye and another his throat; two missed him.

Shortly afterwards, Louis appeared at a window of the Louvre. The crowd gathered below acclaimed him. The young King offered his thanks and exclaimed — 'Now, at this hour, I am King. . .'

SNAKE/EARTH
(you were born in 1905 or 1965)

Earth was born from the slowly falling Elements of the sky at its humid zenith.

Characteristics of the Snake/Earth

This is an afternoon Earth, the humid and hot Earth of summer. It is the symbol of the well-cushioned soft nest, of comfort and abundance; it is an Earth of slow and profound transformation.

This Earth is blessed for the Snake, inviting rest, meditation and revery; it is an Earth of reflection in which everything germinates, ripens, strengthens and dies. A refuge, lair and solitary retreat, it shelters fairy-lands and monsters. The Snake will feel secure, far from the trials and aggressions of the outside world, and will tend to turn in on himself and coil up under this Earth which invites him to relax, even to be inactive. This Element will be protective and soothing, inciting the Snake to idleness and passivity. Yet he cannot live continually underground: he needs sun, air and humidity. Prolonged hibernation would reduce him to a squeaking rodent.

Health of the Snake/Earth

The Earth's organ is the spleen; its flavour is sweet. The Snake/Earth should not remain inactive; he needs fresh air.

He must summon up a certain aggressiveness to stimulate him if he is to maintain his charm.

The Snake/Earth and others

He will be prudent and circumspect, not getting involved lightly, weighing everything carefully and studying the terrain. Distrustful and suspicious by nature, he will be a gifted speculator and a prudent manager, slowly, surely and meticulously amassing wealth — sometimes by debatable means — and adept at concealing it. He has a sense of responsibility and admirably fulfils his role as head of the family, although at times he can be slightly despotic.

Advice for a Snake/Earth

You are often a stay-at-home: go out, communicate with others and keep up with the times; do not close yourself up in your dreams or your past. Put an end to your anxiety and, above all, to old habits — conventional bachelors and spinsters are not attractive. If you cannot overcome your distrust in the business world, at least make an effort to open up on a human level, especially on an emotional one. You will enjoy your success, for you can then breathe security while remaining creative.

A Snake/Earth year

The culminating point of a Snake/Earth year is summer. Summer is favourable for the Snake: free from all material constraints, discover the joys of creation, research and study. But do not close yourself up; leave your hole, come out from underneath the stone and take a sun — not a sleeping — cure. Be more sure of yourself, reach further towards the world and the people in it.

Historical example of a Snake/Earth year 1905

In 1904 Admiral Sir John Fisher returned to the English Admiralty as First Sea Lord. The following year Earl Cawdor was appointed his political associate, the First Lord of the Admiralty. Their collaboration, although only lasting nine months, was memorable.

In 1905 Cawdor and Fisher planned for a war they considered likely if not inevitable. Fisher recognized that the great German admiral, Tirpitz, was building a fleet to fight the British navy. Given the intense jealousy of England felt by the Germans engaged in shipping and in foreign trade, and the rapidly increasing influence of these men over German policy, Fisher and Cawdor both understood that the British fleet should be concentrated in home waters and the traditional 'far flung' dispositions abandoned. To camouflage his plan Fisher took half of the Mediterranean fleet from Malta and based it in Gibraltar. There it could operate into the Atlantic. With Cawdor's backing, Fisher laid down the prototypes for England's future battle fleet, the battleship *Dreadnought* and the battle cruiser *Invincible*. Their construction made obsolete not only every British warship but also those of the German fleet. More important, the vast displacements of the new ships far exceeded the dimensions of the Kiel Canal through which any German ships of a comparable size would have to pass. Thus, Britain could build and equip a fleet of between 10 and 14 battleships before a single German ship of their class could be completed.

Politically, this programme was pacific in intention. Cawdor argued that with such a lead against them the Germans would give up the race. Thus war could be averted. However the Campbell-Bannerman government of 1906 was to throw the lead away, a typical 'liberal' measure which incited the Germans to rectify the balance. Furthermore, the Germans greatly improved on the British prototypes, particularly in the field of optics for gunnery and the protection of magazines. When the test came in 1916 the Royal Navy had only one advantage; its ships were accustomed to the sea. Fisher's and Cawdor's creative work had largely been nullified.

SNAKE/METAL
(you were born in 1929)

In the sky, coming from the West, drought grazed the skin of the Earth and gave birth to Metal.

Characteristics of the Snake/Metal

Metal is of the night, of autumn and of cold. It symbolizes clarity, purity and precision. Its tendency is to be cutting, rigid and chaste; its comments harsh. The Snake/Metal will oscillate between beauty and destruction.

Alas, too much stiffness engenders sadness and moroseness. The Snake/Metal to an extent will be protected by his Element, for it is a veritable armour, shielding him from external danger; but not from internal danger, since it also will exclude the sounds and perfumes, feelings and sensations vital to his inner life. Metal will cool the Snake's warm blood, tending to harden him and make him rigid at the cost of his suppleness and intuition. Imagine a Snake that is completely stiff — he would break in two. Moreover, he will be attracted to an inaccessible and pure ideal which will merely bind him in an even more dogmatic rigidity. Pierce a hole in your handsome armour, let in a little oxygen and dream — you need it.

Health of the Snake/Metal

The organ of Metal is the lung; its flavour is pungent. Breathe deeply, seek the open air, sail or climb a mountain; avoid burrowing or deep-sea diving — at least psychologically.

The Snake/Metal and others

The Snake/Metal will be an energetic man — a military officer, top-level government official, judge or priest — all those professions which are regarded as 'serious'. He will always be just, upright, scrupulous and honest; but he will sometimes be fanatical, due to his love of purity. Loving work that is well-done, expecting and demanding perfection in his own work, he will be pitiless with others, particularly those whom he loves and respects. Clear-sighted and perhaps suffering from his own demands on himself, he is much too proud to recognize his faults and will continue unflaggingly on his way, afraid of letting his resolve be weakened.

Advice for the Snake/Metal

You take yourself too seriously. Be less serious and grave — learn to smile a little. Try to be more humorous, for humour is the best defence against dramas and calamity.

A Snake/Metal year

The culminating point for a Snake/Metal year will be autumn. The Yin tendency of the midseason will unite with the Yang of the Snake, bringing moderation and equilibrium.

Profit from the alternation of Yin and Yang to rediscover your ancestral suppleness; release your armour and relax morally and physically. You have everything to gain, for rigidity is not a necessary element in governing; learn that relaxation and suppleness do not signify weakness.

Historical example of a Snake/Metal year 1809

Defeated in three successive wars and humiliated by the Austerlitz campaign of 1805, the Hapsburgs determined on a war to the finish. They had much to avenge, many humiliations to efface. In the spring of 1809 the signs were propitious. Despite the grave effects on England of Napoleon's 'Continental system' its subsidies were still available. The French armies, embroiled in the Iberian peninsula at deadly cost, appeared over-extended, deployed as they were throughout Europe and along the entirety of its coasts to help enforce the blockade of British goods to

Europe. The British also promised diversionary attacks if a new Continental offensive was launched. The Russians, having recovered from Tilsit, were again menacing Poland and in Italy the French had suffered some rough handling from Austrian troops. Moreover, Napoleon's immediate army consisted only of inexperienced conscripts stiffened by troops from the confederation of the Rhine. Any military appreciation would favour an Austrian offensive.

Yet these appraisals proved worthless. A brief four-day campaign disposed of the army of the Austrian Archduke; two weeks later the French army entered Vienna. His first army lost, the Archduke resorted to his second, carefully held in reserve. He contested Napoleon's attempted crossing of the Danube honourably, but forced to battle at Wagram his army was routed and with it the hopes and expectations of the Hapsburgs. The Emperor concluded an armistice bringing an end to a campaign which had lost him one quarter of his estates and decimated his treasury.

Napoleon required more. He demanded and obtained the hand of the Emperor's 18 year old daughter in marriage. By this alliance the Austrian defeat was cemented.

Analogical Table of the Different Elements

Elements	Wood	Fire	Earth	Metal	Water
Years ending in	3 and 8	2 and 7	0 and 5	4 and 9	1 and 6
Colours	Green	Red	Yellow	White	Blue
Seasons	Spring	Summer	End of summer	Autumn	Winter
Climates	Wind	Heat	Humid	Dry	Cold
Flavours	Acid	Bitter	Sweet	Pungent	Salty
Principal organ	Liver	Heart	Spleen	Lungs	Kidneys
Secondary organ	Gallbladder	Small intestine	Stomach	Large intestine	Bladder
Food	Wheat, poultry	Rice, lamb	Corn, beef	Oats, horse	Peas, pork

Table of Harmony
Between the Elements

	Wood Female	Fire Female	Earth Female	Metal Female	Water Female
Male Wood	●●	○	○○○	○	○○
Male Fire	○	○	○○	●	●●
Male Earth	●●	○○	○○	○○○	●
Male Metal	○	●●	●	●●	○○○
Male Water	○○	●●	●	○○○	○

○○○ Excellent prosperity

○○ Good harmony, understanding

○ Effort needed

● Rivalries and problems of reciprocal domination

●● Misunderstanding and incomprehension

THE
FOUR SEASONS
OF
THE SNAKE

四季

If you were born in spring

Snake/Aries

An extremely contradictory personality: on the one hand we find the less-effort-the-better philosophy of the Snake; on the other, the love of action-for-its-own-sake of Aries. The person marked by this combination is likely to behave unpredictably and suffer rude awakenings. One must not tread on his toes, for he is above all jealous of his independence. He lives at his own rhythm (a euphemism), and is charming if given free-rein materially and emotionally. In this case, he will always return home. But if he is nagged, bothered or bored, he will leave. It is best to accept this in advance.

The Snake/Aries often thinks faster than he acts, but he is very creative. He could become a talented artist, but in practical terms he has a tendency to rely on luck and wait for providence to fill his wallet. Lacking perseverence, he will alter his course whenever he has the impression that he is not getting somewhere. Of all the Snakes he is perhaps the least attracted to difficulties, the most sanely and amiably egotistical — and the most frank.

Snake/Taurus

Charming and a stay-at-home, this Snake loves to warm himself in the sun. His digestion is slow; he is not especially active and does not like to be pushed, being unequalled in his inevitable reply of 'what's the hurry, there's no fire' — he always has time. He is believed to be smug and indifferent. Be careful: the Snake/Taurus is realistic and extremely clear-sighted where his personal comfort is concerned. If it is a question of preserving or improving it, he will stretch, coil to spring and his attack will be as natural and inevitable as the rising tide.

The Snake/Taurus's skin is thick and solid and his personality resistant; but, being also materialistic and acquisitive, he is likely to lose sleep if his shares drop a point or two on the stock exchange (currency devaluation could bring on a depression).

In private he is agreeable and affectionate. Rather faithful for a Snake, he is also horribly jealous and an easier prey for rage than any Othello; the most innocent glance by his companion towards someone else makes him ill. Beware: he may take ten years to react, but when he does he will become wildly furious. Then nothing can stop him, and he will charge like an enraged elephant. If you want to be unfaithful to a Snake/Taurus, be secretive, otherwise buy yourself a coat of armour.

Snake/Gemini

He is rather turbulent for a Snake, but his bite is not fatal. He is not unkind, and if he hurts another's feelings it is always for emotional reasons. In fact, he cannot be held in check: he is inconstant, undisciplined and so sinuous that it is difficult to know where he begins and where he ends. He literally slips between one's fingers.

Emotionally the Snake/Gemini is difficult to live with, but his company is enriching. He is intelligent, intuitive and brilliant, and manipulates his ideas like a magician with his props. He is capable of selling refrigerators to Eskimos or fur coats to the Arabs. Nothing is impossible for him; he loves to convince, to persuade and seduce, which is why he fascinates and twines round Little Red Riding Hoods.

The Snake/Gemini has only to choose. All routes are open to him, particularly those calling for cleverness, diplomacy and eloquence; but working in a coal mine or on the docks is not for him, for he is physically weak.

If you were born in summer
Snake/Cancer

This Snake is sensitive, susceptible and slightly egocentric. He takes himself to be the centre of the world and can quietly doze for hours at a time, coiled about himself. No-one is lazier than a Snake/Cancer: he finds a profound pleasure in doing nothing, nonchalantly stretching himself, savouring his well-being and contemplating the passing hours. If you suddenly rush at him he will turn mean or close himself up like an oyster — on your fingers. He has a great deal of imagination and remarkable intuition, and he is understanding. The Snake/Cancer is efficient, tenacious and opportunistic, thinks out his projects well in advance and is good in a crisis. That dealt with, he will fall asleep again. He is not made for solitary or constricting jobs, but he does a great deal of work without seeming to take much trouble. This sometimes makes others jealous of him.

Extremely attached to his family, the Snake/Cancer is at his best in intimate surroundings; at his own fireside, surrounded by those he loves, listening serenely to the tempest raging outside, he blossoms. Do not worry about his future: he will never lack for anything. If he has no good reason to be active, he will allow himself to be supported with the greatest of pleasure.

Snake/Leo

This is a handsome alliance, for the conquering energy of Leo dynamically influences the contemplative side of the Snake; and the intelligence of the latter diminishes the defects of the Lion, who, among other things, tends to be authoritarian and to take himself too seriously. The Snake/Leo is a man worth consulting. He reflects before acting, and is not discouraged by obstacles. Strong-willed, he is courageous, well-balanced and adaptable. Be careful: he may seem discreet and modest, but in fact conceals a need for power; he still needs to be number one and to be listened to with wide-eyed admiration. This need for reassurance is his weak point for, at bottom, he only wants to be loved.

Ambitious and hating privation, he generally earns enough money to pay for his pleasures. He is at home living in luxury and is capable of creating it. Luck is often with him, for the days are hot in August and it is good for the Snake to be born in fine, warm weather.

Snake/Virgo

These two signs are outstanding for their organizational ability. The Snake/Virgo does not go just anywhere: he knows very well what direction to take. He is so wise that his capacity for almost always being right can become annoying. Luckily, like all Snakes, he is charming. One can feel secure with him because he is faithful to his way of life and enterprises, to his promises, and always keeps his word.

The Snake/Virgo is often cerebral: he reflects a great deal, is clear-sighted and unequalled in avoiding pitfalls. Of course he makes mistakes, but he manages to keep them hidden; he reveals only what he wishes. Always elegant and beautifully dressed, he never swears or uses bad language in public. But at bottom he is nervous and anxious. Sexual equilibrium is of great importance to him. Deceived in love, he becomes ill-tempered and vindictive, revealing a disposition as poisonous as it initially seemed tolerant.

If you were born in autumn
Snake/Libra

If you have ever met up with a Snake/Libra and have been able to resist his charm, you deserve a medal. This Snake is irresistibly seductive and adores pleasing others. He seduces quietly and sinuously, without seeming to touch his prey, who gaze at him, fascinated.

Acutely sensitive to harmony, refined and aesthetic, the Snake/Libra is not aggressive and sometimes needs to be shaken up a bit to prevent him from indulging in daydreams. He is uncertain, hesitant and rather impulsive. He will respond best if you appeal to his sense of justice and his love of peace — in the noblest sense of these terms. An apostle of nonviolence, he will be capable of tirelessly preserving a certain 'quality of life'. Note well: the Snake/Libra does not make jokes about honour.

Snake/Scorpio

The pairing of these two venomous beasts seems dangerous

enough to make one hesitate before stretching out a hand towards them. Luckily however, the Snake/Scorpio is only moderately aggressive and turns it mostly against himself. He only bites or scratches if faced with unjustified meannesss and is actually rather tolerant, for his exceptional perceptiveness enables him to understand the motives of others. He is a good psychologist and would voluntarily spend his evenings investigating the psyches of his colleagues, philosophizing or being introspective.

Tormented and anxious beneath a peaceful exterior, he often changes his skin to mark the deep existential crises in his life. Yet the Snake/Scorpio is endowed with a fundamental strength of will which always enables him to attain his goals, which, being naturally reticent, he does with discretion. Vindictive as an elephant and possessive as a boa constrictor, he likes to be treated with respect. The best approach is to discuss problems with him openly. But if exposed to an accomplished fact, his pride will be hurt and he will enclose himself within his coils. If you come across him ten years later, do not be surprised if he bites you.

Snake/Sagittarius

A dynamic Snake. Although he has no wish to win the Olympic medal for running, he crawls fast enough to attain his end. The Snake's perceptiveness, intuition and sense of organization prevent the Sagittarian personality from thowing him into mad undertakings and keeping bad company. Highly independent, the Snake/Sagittarius is civilized enough to be relatively tolerant of the behaviour of his friends. But be careful: he is something of a stickler about his moral principles and will not accept the idea that one can play around with them. He is an honest man.

He is also authoritarian and slightly intrusive, always ready to inundate you with advice you have not asked for, then crushing you with abuse and contempt if you have the bad taste not to follow it. The Snake/Sagittarius hates to be contradicted, and if you disagree with him, he will bite.

The Snake/Sagittarius is a realist and cannot resist the tinkling of coins. He has a 'treasure-seeking' side and is irritatingly lucky. When he leaves on a search for some Eldorado, you can follow him in total security: you will not end up sleeping under bridges. But do not assume that he will share his treasure with you. That could be risky, for his generosity is relative. He adores giving presents, but is tight-fisted with his money.

If you were born in winter
Snake/Capricorn

He is a self-controlled animal who, behind a peaceful exterior, controls his emotions and looks at the world with impressive lucidity. His glance has the sharpness of a laser beam. He sometimes takes time to decide what action is necessary but, when he does venture forth, you can be sure that his decision is the right one. A Snake/Capricorn does not have time to make mistakes — an entire lifetime will barely suffice for him to obtain what he desires. Born to conquer summits, persevering and obstinate, he does not seem to have heard of the word discouragement. He is without doubt the most resistant of the Snakes, but he does not enjoy himself — make no mistake about it, he has weightier preoccupations.

If a Snake/Capricorn has decided to seduce you, it is useless to buy an aeroplane ticket for Timbuctoo or to lock yourself up in your house. You will only further inspire him in his desire for conquest. He will never be the first to give up and no difficulty will discourage him; he will use all means in his power to catch you. It is almost impossible to resist a Snake/Capricorn. Moreover, although he is not easy to live with, being demanding and egocentric, he does have compensating qualities: he has a remarkable business sense and does not change his opinion every five minutes; he makes one feel extremely secure; also, he is endowed with a rare form of chilly humour and irony. A truly great Snake.

Snake/Aquarius

A plumed Snake, who lives slightly in the clouds or in a Utopia. He is probably the least materialistic of the Snakes, and earning his daily bread is not his main preoccupation. On the other hand, he is remarkably intuitive, humane and available. He has 'antennae', and reacts with deep emotion to the smallest cry for help.

This Snake has the makings of a scholar or genius inventor; he can also make a fortune in peddling the occult or in areas dealing with investigations of the human spirit. Daily details bore him, and if you bother him about paying end-of-the-month bills, taxes and other such financial matters, he will take off in a flying saucer. He must be allowed to give free-rein to his original and creative spirit; but he needs assistance in channelling himself, for he is slightly erratic.

The Snake/Aquarius often has problems in his love life, for he has difficulty reconciling his need of independence with the emotional demands of others. Although sensual — like all Snakes — he is always thinking of other things, and can be sometimes stupidly jealous, at others vexingly indifferent. Luckily, he is so understanding that one can always find some common ground with him — but you must not try to corner him.

Snake/Pisces

Here is an extremely sinuous mixture and, by turning in circles or swimming between two pools, the Snake/Pisces risks biting his own tail and living within the vicious circle of his imagination. He has difficulty knowing what he really wants, and the multiplicity of his talents does not make his choice easy. Even if it seems a pity, he needs to be put firmly on the track. He will never beat any speed records and will sometimes get lost in the countryside; but he will always end up by doing something interesting. Very receptive and remarkably perceptive, this Snake is supple, adaptable and opportunistic. He organizes himself with deceptive ease, never giving the impression of doing so, and always lands on his feet. If crossed the Snake/Pisces will become sullen and inert, poisoning the atmosphere. Happily, he is not too touchy — or else he rarely listens.

Emotionally he risks sinking into melodrama; he rejoices in crimes of passion. He lives great and ever-complicated passions, asks himself far too many questions and exaggerates everything. In an earlier incarnation, he probably lived through *Gone With the Wind*.

At least he is amusing; one is never bored with him. But an entire lifetime is needed to obtain from him one single, precise answer to any question.

THE
I CHING

易经

THE I CHING AND THE SNAKE

In the I Ching game, you ask a question and you obtain an answer. It is therefore a divining game. But the question you ask is posed through your Snake identity; the wheels, the complex mechanism of your mind and spirit, begin to turn. You ask a Snake question and the I Ching answers with a Snake 'solution', on which you then meditate as a Snake before arriving at a Snake conclusion.

The player is presented with a hexagram which contains the 'hypothesis-response' to his question, or, more exactly, a synthesis of forces affecting the concern or event inquired about.

For you, Master Snake, here are the sixty-four hexagrams of the I Ching and sixty-four Snake hypotheses.

How to proceed
1. The question
Ask a question regarding any problem at all, past, present or future, personally concerning you. (If the question concerns a friend, consult the I Ching game in the book corresponding to his Chinese sign.)

2. Method of play
It must be done with concentration.
Take **three ordinary and similar coins** — for example, three 50p coins.
Heads will equal the number 3.
Tails will equal the number 2.
Throw the coins.
If the result is two coins showing Heads and one Tails, write 3 + 3 + 2. You thus obtain a total of 8 which you represent by a continuous line: ——— .
Draw the same continuous line if you have three coins showing Heads (3 + 3 + 3 = 9).

If you throw two coins showing Tails and one Heads (2 + 2 + 3 = 7), or all three showing Tails (2 + 2 + 2 = 6), draw two separate lines: ▬ ▬ .

To sum up, 8 and 9 correspond to: ▬▬▬ (Yin)

6 and 7 correspond to: ▬ ▬ (Yang)

Repeat this operation *six times*, noting at the time of each throw the figure obtained on a piece of paper, proceeding from the first to the sixth figure, from bottom to top.

The final result, including a trigram from the bottom, or lower trigram (example: ▬▬), and a trigram of the top, or upper trigram (example: ▬▬), will be a hexagram of the I Ching. In our example this would look like:

Now merely look for the hexagram number in the table on page 80 , and then consult the list of hexagrams with their descriptions to find the given answer. *In our example,* the hexagram obtained is number 63, entitled **After completion.**

Table of Hexagrams

Trigrams	Upper lines ☰	☷	☳
Lower lines			
☰	1	11	34
☷	12	2	16
☳	25	24	51
☵	6	7	40
☶	33	15	62
☴	44	46	32
☲	13	36	55
☱	10	19	54

Use this table to find the number of your hexagrams. The meeting point between the lower and upper trigrams indicates the number of the hexagram that you are seeking.

☷	☶	☴	☲	☱
5	26	9	14	43
8	23	20	35	45
3	27	42	21	17
29	4	59	64	47
39	52	53	56	31
48	18	57	50	28
63	22	37	30	49
60	41	61	38	58

THE HEXAGRAMS OF THE SNAKE

CH'IEN

1 *The creative:* Energy, strength and will, used and controlled according to the time and hour, will favour that creation dear to the prince of sinuous movement.

K'UN

2 *The receptive:* Having allied yourself with time, recoup your strength by returning to Mother Earth. See things in their proper perspective, watch, retreat, and remember that the night brings advice.

CHUN

3 *Initial difficulty:* Do not blame your disappointments on external circumstances. Do not stubbornly continue to sow wheat in a swamp.

MÊNG

4 *Youthful folly:* 'It is not I who seeks the young fool, but the young fool who seeks me.' You are capable of deep thought and reflection; do not allow yourself to be overcome by your speculative powers, and do not take yourself too seriously.

HSÜ

5 *Waiting:* It is your principal ally, your superior quality, your trump card! The more things stir round you, the more it will be in your best interest to remain immobile.

SUNG

6 *Conflict:* If you are sure of being right, this is not the moment to swish your venom round in your mouth. Be careful: knowing how to give way before a towering obstacle is sometimes wise.

SHIH

7 *The army:* Although you are a passionate individualist, you should bend before discipline and feign submission.

PI

8 *Holding together (union):* Take trouble with your friends and colleagues and carefully knot your coils.

SHIAO CH'U

9 *The taming power of the small:* Scorn nothing, underestimate nothing. Do not qualify anything as 'small' before being certain that you are not near-sighted.

LÜ

10 *Treading:* 'Walk on the tail of the Tiger, he does not bite Man.' Even if you turn green with envy under your scales, do not hiss at the sight of stripes. Be a good prince; a little more prudence and generosity.

T'AI

11 *Peace:* All hostility calms down under its kindly reign. Do not stand on your dignity; draw closer to those you love without reserve; be kind and gentle.

P'I

12 *Standstill:* Is useful before attacking. Control your trembling, draw in your fangs and venom; step back, but remain vigilant.

T'UNG JÊN

13 *Fellowship with men:* Fresh air and daylight are good, and not only for relaxing in the sun. Seek to communicate; open yourself up more to the world and to others; avoid mental reservations.

TA YU

14 *Possession in great measure:* The Snake is lucky as long as he takes trouble and is not satisfied with hatching happiness as though it were a rare egg.

CH'IEN

15 *Modesty:* The Snake is the symbol of the horizontal, but in the case of aggression he rears up and becomes vertical. Guard this option even in difficult trials.

YÜ

16 *Enthusiasm:* It is true that you attract, astonish and confuse, but you are going to be forced to give of yourself without expecting anything in return.

SUI

17 *Following:* The fruits of your work or of your seductiveness will be opened to you; do not become too euphoric.

KU

18 *Work on what has been spoiled:* Buy spectacles or contact lenses. Rule out flirtation; you must look directly and closely at the situation.

LIN

19 *The approach:* Should be slow and prudent, for when the sun burns too brightly, a storm is threatening. Multiply your precautions.

KUAN

20 *Contemplation:* A slightly narcissistic period. Be careful not to turn round in circles; do not forget the world about you and its daily demands.

SHIH HO

21 *Biting through (or clearly defined penalties):* Show all your teeth to discourage your enemies and to force destiny. Throw light on lies and you will eliminate the obstacle.

PI

22 *Grace:* Do not allow yourself to be trapped; that which glitters is not always the light. If you receive a gift, do not throw it into the dustbin while keeping the wrapping.

PO

23 *Splitting apart:* Do not buy a house in which termites have eaten away at the beams. Do not trust appearances too much.

FU

24 *Return — the turning point:* Open your doors and curtains; the sun has risen, the crisis is over and you can go out with complete serenity.

WU WANG

25 *Innocence:* The intuitive Snake can trust completely in his intuition; but he must remain honest and gamble carefully, in case he might be mistaken.

TA CH'U

26 *The taming power of the great:* Power and strength. The Snake changes his skin, renews himself and sloughs off. Do the same if you wish to maintain your force and energy.

I

27 *The corners of the mouth:* Snakes are not all boa constrictors. Do not allow yourself to have eyes bigger than your stomach, nor a head filled with conceit — simply a wisely-filled one.

TA KUO

28 *Preponderance of the great:* Know how to reduce the surplus weight which slows down your sinuous advance.

K'AN

29 *The fathomless water:* External menace. Do not rear up or coil up; continue tranquilly but discreetly on your way, without attracting attention.

LI

30 *The clinging, fire:* Remain calm and do not forever be on guard if you hope to be effective when the time comes. Become involved with people and, when you are alone, commune with nature, for she will help you.

HSIEN

31 *Influence:* You are fascinated and you fascinate, so do not put off your projects until tomorrow. A piece of advice: do not circle round people and things too much before making up your mind.

HÊNG

32 *Duration:* Examine yourself a bit from the inside; internal mutations are also necessary to good equilibrium.

TUN

33 *The retreat:* Retire quietly, as you have the art of doing, discreetly and without making a sound; this is not flight but wisdom.

TA CHUANG

34 *The power of the great:* Strength added to movement. Do not allow yourself to be carried away by the whirlwind, for you would lose control over what surrounds you, as well as over yourself.

CHIN

35 *Progress:* Do not hesitate to assert yourself, show yourself, to make yourself known, but not for very long. Agree to collaborate; the cake should be shared, so do not be too greedy.

MING I

36 *The darkening of the light:* Do not wait for the electrician, but change the fuses yourself. However, learn too how to move round in the dark; you will easily acquire the habit, and the shadows within you, like the clouds, will disappear.

CHIA JÊN

37 *The family:* Even when you are an unfaithful Snake, at least you have the assurance of your family. When you feel lonely, it makes you feel secure; you would do well to make the effort to be responsible to it and not merely resort to it in periods of dire necessity.

K'UEI

38 *Opposition:* Tastes and colours are not arguable; they are discovered. You must try to understand them. Do not adopt or reject them without reflection.

CHIEN

39 *Obstruction:* If you no longer see anything, buy some spectacles; it is useless to continue to grope your way along, which could even become dangerous. If a hand is held out to you, do not refuse it — perhaps there is one more step you have not seen.

HSIEH

40 *Deliverance:* The storm has passed; set things to rights but also leave your shell.

SUN

41 *Decrease:* In case of difficulty, rediscover simplicity. Put your trust in what is spontaneous and natural; life will become gayer.

I

42 *Increase:* This is the moment to act, the barometer points to the 'good weather' sign.

KUAI

43 *Breakthrough:* You can attack and, for once, it will be justifiable; your honesty will shine openly. Hold your head high and denounce error; you are in the limelight.

KOU

44 *Coming to meet:* The Snake is no stranger to sleeping waters, but he should be on his guard and more prudent. Although marshes are a part of his universe, he should not choose them as meeting places.

TS'UI

45 *Gathering together:* Should unite men of all categories and of the most diverse ideas. Seek comradeship but beware of parasites.

SHÊNG

46 *Pushing upwards:* You are sure of yourself; you can leave. But prepare your itinerary, attend carefully to your voyage, neglect no detail and be careful to note the time of departure.

K'UN

47 *Oppression:* You are losing speed; your magnetic fluid has stopped flowing; you must reflect on your conduct.

CHING

48 *The well:* It is good to change, transform and slough off; but renewal does not require destruction.

KO

49 *Revolution:* Is sometimes necessary; build barricades and so prepare yourself for an eventual confrontation.

TING

50 *The cauldron:* Symbolizes the five Elements — Earth, Wood, Fire, Water and Metal — the nourishment of the body and spirit. Know how to find a balance between your spiritual and your material needs.

CHÊN

51 *The arousing (shock, thunder):* Sometimes a nasty jolt can throw light on a subject. Do not make a drama of it, apply a compress and continue on your way — it will perhaps be better illuminated.

KÊN

52 *Keeping still:* Solitude is often a good advisor; for the present be calm and live amid serene surroundings.

CHIEN

53 *Development (gradual progress):* It is more prudent to climb the steps one by one than to bound up them four at a time, risking a fall.

KUEI MEI

54 *The bride:* The Snake who hypnotizes should not himself succumb, but should remain prudent and reflective no matter what happens.

FÊNG

55 *Abundance:* Prosperity and plentitude. The grass is green and the cherry trees are in flower; do not wait for the grass to turn yellow and the flowers to fade to profit from what life has to offer.

LÜ

56 *The wanderer:* Voyages mould youth, calm passions and soothe grief. Step back for a proper perspective, but also look at what lies behind you.

SUN

57 *The gentle:* The wave ceaselessly caresses the shore and, seeping in, wears away the hardest of rocks.

TUI

58 *The serene, the joyous:* Seek to discover the other bank. If you do not like to swim, build a bridge.

HUAN

59 *Dissolution:* Seek to better perceive and understand those about you. Leave your egotism in the cloakroom.

CHIEH

60 *Limitation:* Although guard-rails are useful and practical, do not impose too narrow limits upon yourself or you will find yourself in a rut.

CHUNG FU

61 *Inner truth:* Do not seek to convey what is incapable of transmission. It is your attitude alone which must convince. Do not raise your voice, determined to be heard, but be profound and sincere.

HSIAO KUO

62 *Preponderance of the small:* If you cannot swim, do not jump into the water, especially without a life-jacket.

CHI CHI

63 *After completion:* Know how to admire the blossoming of the rose and detect its fading in the folds of its petals.

WEI CHI

64 *Before completion:* Do not crown yourself with laurels before the prizes are awarded.

General table of the years corresponding to the Chinese signs

THE RAT
31.1.1900/18.2.1901
18.2.1912/ 5.2.1913
5.2.1924/24.1.1925
24.1.1936/10.2.1937
10.2.1948/28.1.1949
28.1.1960/14.2.1961
15.2.1972/ 2.2.1973
2.2.1984/19.2.1985

THE OX
19.2.1901/ 7.2.1902
6.2.1913/25.1.1914
25.1.1925/12.2.1926
11.2.1937/30.1.1938
29.1.1949/16.2.1950
15.2.1961/ 4.2.1962
3.2.1973/22.1.1974
20.2.1985/ 8.2.1986

THE TIGER
8.2.1902/28.1.1903
26.1.1914/13.2.1915
13.2.1926/ 1.2.1927
31.1.1938/18.2.1939
17.2.1950/ 5.2.1951
5.2.1962/24.1.1963
23.1.1974/10.2.1975
9.2.1986/28.1.1987

THE RABBIT
29.1.1903/15.2.1904
14.2.1915/ 2.2.1916
2.2.1927/22.1.1928
19.2.1939/ 7.2.1940
6.2.1951/26.1.1952
25.1.1963/12.2.1964
11.2.1975/30.1.1976
29.1.1987/16.2.1988

THE DRAGON
16.2.1904/ 3.2.1905
3.2.1916/22.1.1917
23.1.1928/ 9.2.1929
8.2.1940/26.1.1941
27.1.1952/13.2.1953
13.2.1964/ 1.2.1965
31.1.1976/17.2.1977
17.2.1988/ 5.2.1989

THE SNAKE
4.2.1905/24.1.1906
23.1.1917/10.2.1918
10.2.1929/29.1.1930
27.1.1941/14.2.1942
14.2.1953/ 2.2.1954
2.2.1965/20.1.1966
18.2.1977/ 6.2.1978
6.2.1989/26.1.1990

THE HORSE
25.1.1906/12.2.1907
11.2.1918/31.1.1919
30.1.1930/16.2.1931
15.2.1942/ 4.2.1943
3.2.1954/23.1.1955
21.1.1966/ 8.2.1967
7.2.1978/27.1.1979
27.1.1990/14.2.1991

THE GOAT
13.2.1907/ 1.2.1908
1.2.1919/19.2.1920
17.2.1931/ 5.2.1932
5.2.1943/24.1.1944
24.1.1955/11.2.1956
9.2.1967/28.1.1968
28.1.1979/15.2.1980
15.2.1991/ 3.2.1992

THE MONKEY
2.2.1908/21.1.1909
20.2.1920/ 7.2.1921
6.2.1932/25.1.1933
25.1.1944/12.2.1945
12.2.1956/30.1.1957
29.1.1968/16.2.1969
16.2.1980/ 4.2.1981
4.2.1992/22.1.1993

THE ROOSTER
22.1.1909/ 9.2.1910
8.2.1921/27.1.1922
26.1.1933/13.2.1934
13.2.1945/ 1.2.1946
31.1.1957/15.2.1958
17.2.1969/ 5.2.1970
5.2.1981/24.1.1982
23.1.1993/ 9.2.1994

THE DOG
10.2.1910/29.1.1911
28.1.1922/15.2.1923
14.2.1934/ 3.2.1935
2.2.1946/21.1.1947
16.2.1958/ 7.2.1959
6.2.1970/26.1.1971
25.1.1982/12.2.1983
10.2.1994/30.1.1995

THE PIG
30.1.1911/17.2.1912
16.2.1923/ 4.2.1924
4.2.1935/23.1.1936
22.1.1947/ 9.2.1948
8.2.1959/27.1.1960
27.1.1971/14.2.1972
13.2.1983/ 1.2.1984
31.1.1995/18.2.1996

*The dates indicated specify the **first** and the **last** day of the year of the sign.*

THE HANDBOOK OF CHINESE HOROSCOPES

Theodora Lau

Are you a sentimental but crafty Rat, a serious and dutiful Ox, or a capitivating but unpredictable Tiger? Here, in the most comprehensive book ever written on Chinese astrology, you can find out which of the twelve animal signs of the lunar calendar is yours, how your sign is affected by the Yin and Yang, how your Moon sign and your Sun sign affect each other — and which of the other animal signs you're compatible with.

THE BOOK OF CHINESE BELIEFS

Frena Bloomfield

Earth magic, ghost weddings, passports to the after-life, the spirit world of the Chinese exists side-by-side with everyday reality, and affects every aspect of Chinese life from diet and decor to getting married or opening a business.

Frena Bloomfield has lived and worked in Hong Kong and has talked in depth to many practitioners of the magic arts. THE BOOK OF CHINESE BELIEFS is a fascinating introduction to a rich culture where the dead are ever-present and even the siting of a house or village is governed by the laws of earth magic.

HOROSCOPES

Arrow publish an individual Super Horoscope book for each of the twelve signs of the Zodiac, and the definitive *Handbook of Chinese Horoscopes* by Theodora Lau. These books can be bought in your local bookshop or you can order these directly by completing the form below.

SUPER HOROSCOPES 1984

____	**ARIES** (21 March – 20 April)	**£1.50**
____	**TAURUS** (21 April – 20 May)	**£1.50**
____	**GEMINI** (21 May – 20 June)	**£1.50**
____	**CANCER** (21 June – 20 July)	**£1.50**
____	**LEO** (21 July – 20 August)	**£1.50**
____	**VIRGO** (22 August – 22 September)	**£1.50**
____	**LIBRA** (23 September – 22 October)	**£1.50**
____	**SCORPIO** (23 October – 22 November)	**£1.50**
____	**SAGITTARIUS** (23 November – 20 December)	**£1.50**
____	**CAPRICORN** (21 December – 19 January)	**£1.50**
____	**AQUARIUS** (20 January – 18 February)	**£1.50**
____	**PISCES** (19 February – 20 March)	**£1.50**

Also available

____	**HANDBOOK OF CHINESE HOROSCOPES**	**£1.95**
	Postage	_____
	Total	_____

ARROW BOOKS, BOOKSERVICE BY POST, PO BOX 29, DOUGLAS, ISLE OF MAN

Please enclose a cheque or postal order made out to Arrow Books Limited for the amount due including 10p per book for postage and packing within the UK and 12p for overseas orders.

Please print clearly

NAME . . . .

ADDRESS . . . .

. . . .

Whilst every effort is made to keep prices down and to keep popular books in print, Arrow Books cannot guarantee that prices will be the same as those advertised here or that books will be available.